FOOD for THOUGHT

Also from Ellen G. White

God's Nutritionist

FOOD for THOUGHT

Words to Live by from Ellen G. White

Edited by Robert Cohen

SQUAREONE
CLASSICS

Cover Designer: Phaedra Mastrocola and Jeannie Tudor
Typesetter: Gary A. Rosenberg
In-House Editor: Eric Motylinski

Square One Publishers
115 Herricks Road
Garden City Park, NY 11040
(516) 535-2010 • (877) 900-BOOK
www.squareonepublishers.com

Library of Congress Cataloging-in-Publication Data

White, Ellen Gould Harmon, 1827–1915.
  Food for thought : Ellen G. White's healing prophecies / [compiled by] Robert Cohen.
    p. cm.
  ISBN-13: 978-0-7570-0178-9 (quality pbk.)
  ISBN-10: 0-7570-0178-5 (quality pbk.)
  1. White, Ellen Gould Harmon, 1827-1915—Quotations. 2. Seventh-Day Adventists—Doctrines—Quotations, maxims, etc. I. Cohen, Robert. II. Title.

BX6154.W458945 2008
286.7'32—dc22
                        2007041552

Square One Classics is an imprint of Square One Publishers, Inc.

Copyright © 2008 by Robert Cohen

All rights reserved. No part of this publication may be reproduced, stored in a retrieval system, or transmitted, in any form or by any means, electronic, mechanical, photocopying, recording, or otherwise, without the prior written permission of the copyright owner.

10 9 8 7 6 5 4 3 2 1

Contents

Dedication, vii
Foreword, ix
Introduction, 1

Topics

Adversity, 5
Aging, 7
Alcohol, 8
Appearance and Presentation, 10
Baking Bread, 11
Body as a Sanctuary, 12
Breathing for Life, 16
Caring for Children, 19
Caring for the Sick, 21
Charity, 24
Children's Diets, 26
Children's Needs, 28
Cleanliness, 29
Comfort of Home, 32
Compassion for Animals, 34
Compassion for Others, 37
Cooking Healthy Food, 41
Cooking Instructions, 42

Country Living, 44
Determination, 46
Diet and Exercise, 48
Dieting Rules, 50
Diseases, 55
Doctors, 57
Eating Poorly, 60
Eating Properly, 64
Educating Children, 68
Education for Life, 70
Emotions, 72
Exercise for the Body, 73
Faith in God, 75
Faith in Self, 79
Family, 80
Food Dangers, 84
Food for Health, 86
God's Gifts and Love, 87

Happiness, 90	Mothers' Duties, 128
Happy Marriages, 91	Nature, 133
Healing Naturally, 93	Nurses, 137
Home Environment, 98	Optimism, 138
Living Superficially, 100	Parenting Advice, 141
Love, 103	Parenting Wisdom, 144
Marital Advice, 105	Parents Teaching Kids, 147
Meat Consumption, 108	Pessimism, 149
Medicine, 112	Seize the Day, 153
Mental Fitness, 113	Self-Healing, 155
Money, 115	Spending Extravagantly, 157
Morality Between Peers, 116	Strength, 158
Morality in Medicine, 117	Temptation, 159
Morality in Self, 119	Tobacco, 161
Morality in Society, 121	Vices, 164
Mother Appreciation, 124	Working Diligently, 168
Mothers and Children, 126	Note from the Editor, 171

Dedication

To my mother Dorothy, who at eighty-nine regularly plays duplicate bridge with friends two or three generations younger than herself and has accumulated enough points to qualify as a life master.

On my own scorecard, she has always been my master of life, teaching me to cook, to learn, to study, and to turn compassion into action.

There was one day I remember in the late 1950s in New York City when two of my friends and I could not find a fourth for our daily stickball game.

I became mortified when she volunteered, and I still recall a six-year-old's sense of dread when my mother clutched a broomstick and took her first swing. The pink Spalding ball sailed past three sewers. That home run has been frozen in my mind for half a century. It could not have occurred in slow motion, but that is how my mind's eye replays the moment, like a Robert Redford home run in *The Natural*.

As Mom approaches her ninetieth birthday, I pay tribute to the woman who continuously taught me the moral and ethical lessons of life, which have evolved into my own activism, writing, and lectures. In that sense, her touches have changed the world by inspiring my own Ministry of Healing.

Foreword

Ellen White gets it! She understands the twenty-first-century heart-cry to know and experience God, to do something meaningful and enduring in life, and to grapple with issues of poverty, alienation, health, education, diversity, inclusiveness, integrity, and eternity.

Yet she's dead.

No, I haven't been channeling Ellen White. I'm only trumpeting the good news that the principles she espoused transcend time and are more pertinent and applicable today than ever.

But with myriad books on health, spirituality, and lifestyle available today, could Ellen White's voice still have relevance? Robert Cohen says, "Yes!" In this wonderful comparative analysis featuring classical, nineteenth-century, and contemporary authors who wrote on similar topics, Robert Cohen shows that in some cases White's principles are oppositional to those of other wisdom writers, in other cases they mirror them, and in still others they are unique and "fill in the gaps" left by philosophers through the ages. Writing on a plethora of subjects over a period of nearly seventy years, Ellen White promoted principles that are consistent and that remain timeless.

An unexpected result of my own research of Ellen White's writings for my book *Ellen White and Leadership* (Pacific Press) was the discovery of her counsel that leaders should lead by cultivating a relationship with their followers that is based on shared vision, shared values, and shared purpose, and that is characterized by authentic conflict, managed transitions, and sustainable change. How twenty-first-century is that!

Though some of her counsel on knowing God parallels that of other nineteenth-century moralists, evangelists, and theologians who wrote on prayer, Scripture study, and character development, her spiritual counsel nonetheless bears the hallmark of her unique and overarching worldview of the great controversy between Christ and Satan, good and evil. She always looked beyond the present existence to heavenly realities, and her counsel reflects that projection. Likewise, though some of her health and lifestyle counsel reflects ideas of others, she never bought those ideas wholesale. Indeed, her health principles were sometimes completely opposite those of the most popular health reformers of her day. She believed that God and His Spirit—not her own opinions or interpretations—were the source of her inspiration.

I categorize her principles and theories as progressive because she promoted a fresh approach to old truths, because she empowered an inclusive spiritual movement, and because she condemned as conservative those who refused to examine new understandings of Scripture. Additionally, Ellen White's counsel repeatedly defies the metaphors of her own industrial era, where "machine" best described organization—with all of machinery's inherent orderly and rational uniformity, complete with inflexible rules enforced by a rigid system of hierarchy. Against this cultural milieu, Ellen White promoted creativity, appropriate conflict, humanizing interaction with workers, and distributed leadership. She also extolled biblical values (in today's leadership literature, often called "human values") such as spirit, love, empowerment, trust, grace, humility, and forgiveness. Though born into a world of radical individualism, Ellen White nonetheless emphasized a community-based movement. In her well-known book *Education*, she urged leaders to move courageously through complexities of transition and chaos in the certain hope that humans will move beyond the fractal predictability of time, space, and matter when God intervenes in earth history (2 Peter 3:4).

Food for Thought

The metaphor for today's organization is a living system that may be chaotic, complex, creative, unpredictable, and filled with conflicting values. No single individual can bring about sustainable change and progress to a living system in time of great transformation. I found that to be exactly what Ellen White (albeit in nineteenth-century language) is saying! Not only is each leader to consider himself or herself part of a team effort, but that leader must also recognize that his or her success will be in direct proportion to the willingness to be filled with God's spirit.

Perhaps the closest that Ellen White comes to expressing a theory of leadership, time management, or existential purpose can be found in this statement in her book *Our High Calling*:

> Regard every moment of time as golden. Do not waste it in indolence; do not spend it in folly; but grasp the higher treasures. Cultivate the thoughts and expand the soul by girding about the mind, not allowing it to be filled with unimportant matters. Secure every advantage within your reach for strengthening the intellect. Do not be satisfied with a low standard. Do not rest content until by faithful endeavor, watchfulness, and earnest prayer, you have secured the wisdom that is from above. Thus you may rise in character, and gain an influence over other minds, enabling you to lead them in the path of uprightness and holiness. This is your privilege.

Whether they regard Him as teacher, prophet, or Messiah, most cultures value principles from Christ's teachings. Jesus used agrarian society as the backdrop for many of His parables, yet the principles from His stories endure even in societies far removed from the culture to which He originally spoke and despite unprecedented rates of societal evolution. Likewise, Ellen White makes a significant contribution to the discovery and understanding of meaning in life. It does not appear that her principles on health, spirituality, and lifestyle will ever become outdated, even in the face of accelerating world change, because they have universal application. In fact, in the May 30, 2005 edition of its electronic newsletter, *Update,* the Barna Group reported that pastors under the age of forty championed Ellen White as one of their most significant influences in an ever-changing world.

Increasingly powerful economic, political, religious, and social forces, such as the growth in the number of countries linked to the capitalist system and the spread of information networks that connect people globally, may soon be associated with changes most people in the world never envisioned. In this projected milieu, Ellen White's counsel on knowing God and anchoring that knowledge in Scripture may have far more relevance than can be imagined today. Her principles seem to cut through the nebulous maze of theoretic kerfuffle and put the mind and will of God at the center of our choices.

In an era of global information dissemination and commerce, high-speed communication, terrorism, AIDS, and family disintegration, our world may seem radically different from Ellen White's. Yet perhaps it is *because* of the accelerating rate of change in our world that her counsel—to cultivate a calm trust in God in the face of life's stressors and the mercurial movement of societal change—seems surprisingly fresh and apropos.

On few subjects does Ellen White give more counsel than she does on the need to care for the poor, needy, and marginalized. If leaders of our world had no counsel apart from this, Ellen White's enduring legacy and relevance to them would be assured. In the midst of unparalleled prosperity, neglect of the needy corresponds to spiritual poverty. The perpetual search for meaning in the workplace might be resolved if people prioritized Ellen White's counsel about serving the poor, because her counsel contributes significant answers to Tolstoy's important questions—"What shall we do and how shall we live?"

So yes, absolutely—I believe Ellen White's counsel on both spiritual and practical themes has continuing relevance in the twenty-first century. For those like me whose biblical understanding grants Ellen White status as a God-inspired visionary, her counsel doubtless has greater impact than for those who do not

Food for Thought

believe her authority is greater than that of any other devotional writer. Even those in the latter category, however, may find that her spiritual and lifestyle principles sharpen their inner focus and that her practical counsel offers sound injunctions for the often frenetic and conflicted workplace, community, and society. Ellen White's principles could well have a significant impact on all of us, inspiring both compassionate action and a deepening commitment to make healthy physical, spiritual, and mental choices.

Margaret J. Wheatley, in the preface of her own book *Leadership and the New Science: Discovering Order in a Chaotic World*, perhaps aptly summarizes Ellen G. White's leadership counsel when she states, "I realize that the work is not to introduce a few new ideas, but to change a world view." Ellen G. White's counsel and principles may not just change how we think about our world but also revolutionize our priorities and change the entire direction of our lives.

Cindy Tutsch, D.Min
Associate Director
Ellen G. White Estate
Silver Spring, Maryland

Introduction

At the age of seventeen, Ellen G. White experienced her first religious vision. During the course of her lifetime, 2,000 additional revelations were to become a collective prophecy that would lay a hand upon millions of individuals. As a result of her own personal encounters with God, she and her husband, James White, along with Joseph Bates, founded the Seventh-day Adventist (SDA) church.

In her literary career, White authored more than forty books compiled from over 25 million of her written words contained in 50,000 pages of manuscript. Her voluminous work has been published into 140 different languages, making Ellen White the most translated author in the history of American literature. In 1905, at the age of seventy-eight, Ellen G. White distributed what was to become one of her best-known books, *The Ministry of Healing*. In that book, Mrs. White shared her divinely inspired prophecies, which included an appreciation of those fundamentals that would lead to healthy living.

In May of 2003, while doing research for *God's Nutritionist*, I was fortunate to visit the Ellen G. White estate in Silver Spring, Maryland, where many of Mrs. White's original documents are stored in bank-like vaults. Silver Spring is also home to one of the world's largest Adventist health food and book stores. A few hours before my appointment with the SDA archivists, I visited the bookstore. In an effort to avoid 200 miles of snarling rush-

Food for Thought

hour traffic in the New York–Washington corridor, I left my New Jersey home many hours before sunrise. Knowing that I would arrive before the store opened, I brought along newspapers to occupy my waiting time. I was surprised by the size of the store, which occupied an area equivalent to a typical supermarket, and could not resist getting out of the car and doing some window-shopping. There on display were many hundreds of books and vegetarian health foods. In front of the store was a larger-than-life bronze statue of Jesus, washing the feet of his disciple Peter.

The statue was impressive in its lifelike detail, as was the message of foot-washing at its base, citing John 12:1–8 and 13:1–17. I copied down the citations on a piece of paper and folded it into my pocket for later review. I had thirty minutes before the store opened to reflect upon the meaning of what I read. I circled the statue, admiring the sculptor's skill from many angles.

As a young woman, Ellen G. White supported foot-washing as a tradition in the church. That symbolic act is still practiced in many SDA congregations. As a Jew, I was not introduced to foot-washing, although there is some mention of that custom in the Old Testament. In "the beginning" (Genesis 18:4), we find Abraham attending to three visitors by bidding them to wash their feet on a very hot day. Although Abraham supplied the water, he did not do the actual foot-washing. He busied himself by preparing food for his guests. One chapter later (Genesis 19:2), Old Testament readers find Lot rising to greet two angels at the gates of Sodom. He invited his visitors to bathe their feet. So apparently the age-old custom of washing the feet of sandal-wearing desert travelers served both as a primary means of cleaning one's dirty feet and as a way of graciously showing respect by comforting a weary guest.

I was so taken with the imagery of Jesus washing Peter's feet that when a young man arrived to open up the store I jokingly asked whether he wished to wash my own feet. He smiled and politely declined the offer, but he surpassed the obligation of a retailer by giving me a personal tour of the store, explaining the history behind each of Mrs. White's major works. The imagery of

Food for Thought

Jesus washing Peter's feet had made an initial impression upon me. During this tour, I first thought of writing a column or article about the custom of cleaning feet. Although I knew little of the tradition, I recalled stories and visions of Mother Teresa washing the feet of beggars in Calcutta, India. I became fascinated by the loving gesture of foot-washing, and made it a goal to research the subject in the following weeks. During that same period of time I began to read Ellen G. White's *Ministry of Healing*. In recognition of a powerful moment in my life, I went away alone for the weekend to read the book a second time. I began to write in the margins, taking notes on one brilliant observation after another, and then it came to me. Cleansing and purifying souls. That is what White's *Ministry of Healing* is all about.

Ministry of Healing is a primer in childcare and health care, diet and nutrition, schooling, dress, and cleanliness. If one were challenged to write the be-all and end-all to raising a family with plenty of love and strong values, this would be the text. As I read White's words, I felt as if I was reading the most important thoughts and philosophies contained within the great books of Western literature—from Aristotle to Voltaire to Goethe to Emerson; from Shakespeare to Schopenhauer to Freud to Thoreau. Mrs. White's insights are both inspiring and instructional, as are theirs.

Mother Teresa washed feet. Her inspiration was Jesus. During the Passover Seder before His crucifixion, Jesus washed the feet of His disciples as a sign of love and respect. Peter wanted no part of the ceremony, but Jesus made clear to all that such an action was the law of love. Jesus washed Peter's feet that day, and the act of foot-washing is still performed by many twenty-first-century congregations. In cleansing soles, Jesus was purifying souls. In writing *Ministry of Healing,* Ellen White gave the gift of spiritual cleansing to her SDA followers. By setting down rules of hygiene, White purified both soles and souls.

Writing *Food for Thought* was for me an exercise in both knowledge and love. The discovery of quotations from humankind's most brilliant men and women to support Ellen G. White's work took great time and effort. Hundreds of hours of study, reviewing

Food for Thought

tens of thousands of sources during the summer of 2003, resulted in the volume you now hold in your hands. Each one of the nearly 400 different quotations provides a lesson for study and introspection. Together as one, quotations from hundreds of authors, philosophers, respected elders, and other personalities are combined with Ellen G. White's own work. Together, they shimmer like a powerful beacon of truth, with Mrs. White's work as the centerpiece, outshining the brightest of stars.

Food for Thought

ADVERSITY

So long as we are in the world, we shall meet with adverse influences. Day by day and year by year we shall conquer self and grow into a noble heroism. (*Ministry of Healing*, page 487)

> "The harder the conflict, the more glorious the triumph. What we obtain too cheap, we esteem too lightly; it is dearness only that gives everything its value. I love the man that can smile in trouble, that can gather strength from distress and grow brave by reflection."
>
> Thomas Paine

Many have borne so few burdens, their hearts have known so little real anguish, they have felt so little perplexity and distress in behalf of others, that they cannot understand the work of the true burden bearer. No more capable are they of appreciating his burdens than is the child of understanding the care and toil of his burdened father. The child may wonder at his father's fears and perplexities. These appear needless to him. But when years of experience shall have been added to his life, when he himself comes to bear its burdens, he will look back upon his father's life and understand that which was once so incomprehensible. Bitter experience has given him knowledge. (*Ministry of Healing*, page 483)

> "The sudden disappointment of a hope leaves a scar which the ultimate fulfillment of that hope never entirely removes."
>
> Thomas Hardy

Many a widowed mother with her fatherless children is bravely striving to bear her double burden, often toiling far beyond her strength in order to keep her little ones with her and to provide for their needs. Little time has she for their training and

Food for Thought

instruction, little opportunity to surround them with influences that would brighten their lives. She needs encouragement, sympathy, and tangible help. (*Ministry of Healing*, page 203)

> "No man ever sank under the burden of the day. It is when tomorrow's burden is added to the burden of today, that the weight is more than a man can bear."
>
> — George MacDonald

We are in a world of suffering. Difficulty, trial, and sorrow await us all along the way to the heavenly home. But there are many who make life's burdens doubly heavy by continually anticipating trouble. If they meet with adversity or disappointment they think that everything is going to ruin, that theirs is the hardest lot of all, that they are surely coming to want. Thus they bring wretchedness upon themselves and cast a shadow upon all around them. Life itself becomes a burden to them. But it need not be thus. It will cost a determined effort to change the current of their thought. But the change can be made. Their happiness, both for this life and for the life to come, depends upon their fixing their minds upon cheerful things. Let them look away from the dark picture, which is imaginary, to the benefits which God has strewn in their pathway, and beyond these to the unseen and eternal. (*Ministry of Healing*, page 247)

> "Trials teach us what we are; they dig up the soil, and let us see what we are made of."
>
> — Charles Haddon Spurgeon

AGING

So far as possible let those whose whitening heads and failing steps show that they are drawing near to the grave remain among friends and familiar associations. Let them worship among those whom they have known and loved. Let them be cared for by loving and tender hands. (*Ministry of Healing,* page 204)

> "I promise to keep on living as though I expected to live forever. Nobody grows old by merely living a number of years. People grow old only by deserting their ideals. Years may wrinkle the skin, but to give up interest wrinkles the soul."
>
> Douglas MacArthur

Those who have the aged to provide for should remember that these especially need warm, comfortable rooms. Vigor declines as years advance, leaving less vitality with which to resist unhealthful influences; hence the greater necessity for the aged to have plenty of sunlight, and fresh, pure air. (*Ministry of Healing,* page 275)

> "The duty of caring for failing elderly relatives is more than a family matter, a personal dilemma, or a sex equity issue. Basically, it is a problem of how our society views old and disabled people. With the growing numbers of chronically ill, it can no longer be some other family's tragedy. Eventually we must face hard questions, as individuals and as a nation."
>
> Tish Sommers

There is a blessing in the association of the old and the young. The young may bring sunshine into the hearts and lives of the aged. Those whose hold on life is weakening need the benefit of contact with the hopefulness and buoyancy of youth. And the

Food for Thought

young may be helped by the wisdom and experience of the old. (*Ministry of Healing*, page 204)

> "So precious life is! Even to the old the hours are as a miser's coins!"
>
> Thomas Bailey Aldrich

ALCOHOL

Think of the frightful accidents that are every day occurring through the influence of drink. Some official on a railway train neglects to heed a signal or misinterprets an order. On goes the train; there is a collision, and many lives are lost. Or a steamer is run aground, and passengers and crew find a watery grave. When the matter is investigated, it is found that someone at an important post was under the influence of drink. To what extent can one indulge the liquor habit and be safely trusted with the lives of human beings? He can be trusted only as he totally abstains. (*Ministry of Healing*, page 331)

> "Drowning one's sorrows in drink only makes them worse."
>
> Chinese proverb

Some who are never considered really drunk are always under the influence of mild intoxicants. They are feverish, unstable in mind, unbalanced. Imagining themselves secure, they go on and on, until every barrier is broken down, every principle sacrificed. The strongest resolutions are undermined, the highest considerations are not sufficient to keep the debased appetite under the control of reason. (*Ministry of Healing*, page 332)

Food for Thought

"Men fed upon carnage, and drinking strong drinks, have all an impoisoned and acrid blood which drives them mad in a hundred different ways."

Voltaire

Persons who have inherited an appetite for unnatural stimulants should by no means have wine, beer, or cider in their sight, or within their reach; for this keeps the temptation constantly before them. (*Ministry of Healing,* page 331)

"My experience through life has convinced me that, while moderation and temperance in all things are commendable and beneficial, abstinence from spirituous liquors is the best safeguard of morals and health."

Robert E. Lee

Intoxication is just as really produced by wine, beer, and cider as by stronger drinks. The use of these drinks awakens the taste for those that are stronger, and thus the liquor habit is established. Moderate drinking is the school in which men are educated for the drunkard's career. Yet so insidious is the work of these milder stimulants that the highway to drunkenness is entered before the victim suspects his danger. (*Ministry of Healing,* page 332)

"Alcohol is barren. The words a man speaks in the night of drunkenness fade like the darkness itself at the coming of day."

Marguerite Duras

But if the mother unswervingly adheres to right principles, if she is temperate and self-denying, if she is kind, gentle, and unselfish, she may give her child these same precious traits of character. Very explicit was the command prohibiting the use of wine by the mother. Every drop of strong drink taken by her to gratify appetite endangers the physical, mental, and moral health of her child, and is a direct sin against her Creator." (*Ministry of Healing*, page 373)

> "If you are poor, avoid wine as a costly luxury; if you are rich, shun it as a fatal indulgence. Stick to plain water."
>
> Herman Melville

APPEARANCE AND PRESENTATION

But our clothing, while modest and simple, should be of good quality, of becoming colors, and suited for service. It should be chosen for durability rather than display. It should provide warmth and proper protection. The wise woman described in the Proverbs "is not afraid of the snow for her household: for all her household are clothed with double garments." Proverbs 31:21 (*Ministry of Healing*, page 288)

> "In your clothes avoid too much gaudiness; do not value yourself upon an embroidered gown; and remember that a reasonable word, or an obliging look, will gain you more respect than all your fine trappings."
>
> George Savile

The Bible teaches modesty in dress. "In like manner also, that women adorn themselves in modest apparel." (Timothy 2:9). This forbids display in dress, gaudy colors, profuse ornamentation. Any device designed to attract attention to the wearer or to excite

Food for Thought

admiration, is excluded from the modest apparel which God's word enjoins. (*Ministry of Healing*, page 287)

BAKING BREAD

Bread should be light and sweet. Not the least taint of sourness should be tolerated. The loaves should be small and so thoroughly baked that, so far as possible, the yeast germs shall be destroyed. When hot or new, raised bread of any kind is difficult on digestion. It should never appear on the table. This rule does not, however, apply to unleavened bread. Fresh rolls made of wheaten meal without yeast or leaven, and baked in a well-heated oven, are both wholesome and palatable. (*Ministry of Healing*, page 301)

> "If the divine creator has taken pains to give us delicious and exquisite things to eat, the least we can do is prepare them well and serve them with ceremony."
>
> Fernand Point

In the making of raised or yeast bread, milk should not be used in place of water. The use of milk is an additional expense, and it makes the bread much less wholesome. Milk bread does not keep sweet so long after baking as does that made with water, and it ferments more readily in the stomach. (*Ministry of Healing*, page 301)

> "Everybody needs beauty as well as bread, places to play in and pray in, where nature may heal and give strength to body and soul."
>
> John Muir

For use in bread-making, the superfine white flour is not the best. Its use is neither healthful nor economical. Fine-flour bread is lacking in nutritive elements to be found in bread made from the whole wheat. It is a frequent cause of constipation and other unhealthful conditions. (*Ministry of Healing*, page 300)

> "Better is half a loaf than no bread."
>
> John Heywood

BODY AS A SANCTUARY

God is not honored when the body is neglected or abused and is thus unfitted for His service. To care for the body by providing for it food that is relishable and strengthening is one of the first duties of the householder. It is far better to have less expensive clothing and furniture than to stint the supply of food. (*Ministry of Healing*, page 322)

> "My great religion is a belief in the blood, the flesh, as being wiser than the intellect. We can go wrong in our minds. But what our blood feels and believes and says, is always true. The intellect is only a bit and a bridle."
>
> D.H. Lawrence

At every pulsation of the heart the blood should make its way quickly and easily to all parts of the body. Its circulation should not be hindered by tight clothing or bands, or by insufficient clothing of the extremities. Whatever hinders the circulation forces the blood back to the vital organs, producing congestion.

Food for Thought

Headache, cough, palpitation of the heart, or indigestion is often the result. (*Ministry of Healing*, page 271)

> "It is in moments of illness that we are compelled to recognize that we live not alone but chained to a creature of a different kingdom, whole worlds apart, who has no knowledge of us and by whom it is impossible to make ourselves understood: our body."
>
> Marcel Proust

That which corrupts the body tends to corrupt the soul. (*Ministry of Healing*, page 280)

> "The hollow sea-shell, which for years hath stood on dusty shelves, when held against the ear, proclaims its stormy parent, and we hear the faint, far murmur of the breaking flood. We hear the sea. The Sea? It is the blood in our own veins, impetuous and near."
>
> Eugene Lee-Hamilton

Our bodies are built up from the food we eat. There is a constant breaking down of the tissues of the body; every movement of every organ involves waste, and this waste is repaired from our food. Each organ of the body requires its share of nutrition. The brain must be supplied with its portion; the bones, muscles, and nerves demand theirs. It is a wonderful process that transforms the food into blood and uses this blood to build up the varied parts of the body; but this process is going on continually, supplying with life and strength each nerve, muscle, and tissue. (*Ministry of Healing*, page 295)

Food for Thought

> "Regard this body as a machine which, having been made by the hand of God, is incomparably better ordered than any machine that can be devised by man, and contains in itself movements more wonderful than those in any machine. It is for all practical purposes impossible for a machine to have enough organs to make it act in all the contingencies of life in the way in which our reason makes us act."
>
> — René Descartes

The mechanism of the human body cannot be fully understood; it presents mysteries that baffle the most intelligent. It is not as the result of a mechanism, which, once set in motion, continues its work, that the pulse beats and breath follows breath. The beating heart, the throbbing pulse, every nerve and muscle in the living organism, is kept in order and activity by the power of an ever-present God. (*Ministry of Healing*, page 417)

> "Every man is the builder of a temple, called his body, to the god he worships, after a style purely his own, nor can he get off by hammering marble instead. We are all sculptors and painters, and our material is our own flesh and bones. Any nobleness begins at once to refine a man's features, any meanness or sensuality to imbrute them."
>
> — Henry David Thoreau

Too little attention is generally given to the preservation of health. It is far better to prevent disease than to know how to treat it when contracted. It is the duty of every person, for his own sake, and for the sake of humanity, to inform himself in regard to the laws of life and conscientiously to obey them. All need to become acquainted with that most wonderful of all organisms, the human body. They should understand the functions of the various organs and the

Food for Thought

dependence of one upon another for the healthy action of all. They should study the influence of the mind upon the body, and of the body upon the mind, and the laws by which they are governed. (*Ministry of Healing,* page 128)

> "Look to your health; and if you have it, praise God and value it next to conscience; for health is the second blessing that we mortals are capable of, a blessing money can't buy."
>
> Izaak Walton

God has endowed us with a certain amount of vital force. He has also formed us with organs suited to maintain the various functions of life, and He designs that these organs shall work together in harmony. If we carefully preserve the life force, and keep the delicate mechanism of the body in order, the result is health; but if the vital force is too rapidly exhausted, the nervous system borrows power for present use from its resources of strength, and when one organ is injured, all are affected. Nature bears much abuse without apparent resistance; she then arouses and makes a determined effort to remove the effects of the ill-treatment she has suffered. Her effort to correct these conditions is often manifest in fever and various other forms of sickness. (*Ministry of Healing,* page 234)

> "Infirmity doth still neglect all office whereto our health is bound; we are not ourselves when nature, being oppressed, commands the mind to suffer with the body."
>
> William Shakespeare

BREATHING FOR LIFE

In order to have good health, we must have good blood; for the blood is the current of life. It repairs waste and nourishes the body. When supplied with the proper food elements and when cleansed and vitalized by contact with pure air, it carries life and vigor to every part of the system. The more perfect the circulation, the better will this work be accomplished.
(*Ministry of Healing*, page 271)

> A thing of beauty is a joy for ever:
> Its loveliness increases; it will never
> Pass into nothingness; but still will keep
> A bower quiet for us, and a sleep
> Full of sweet dreams, and health, and quiet breathing.
>
> — John Keats

The lungs are constantly throwing off impurities, and they need to be constantly supplied with fresh air. Impure air does not afford the necessary supply of oxygen, and the blood passes to the brain and other organs without being vitalized. Hence the necessity of thorough ventilation. To live in close, ill-ventilated rooms, where the air is dead and vitiated, weakens the entire system. It becomes peculiarly sensitive to the influence of cold, and a slight exposure induces disease. It is close confinement indoors that makes many women pale and feeble. They breathe the same air over and over until it becomes laden with poisonous matter thrown off through the lungs and pores, and impurities are thus conveyed back to the blood. (*Ministry of Healing*, page 274)

Food for Thought

"Today, I want you to notice how you're breathing throughout the day. This simple activity can tell you the state of your nervous system—and by learning to control your breathing, you can influence the regulation of your heart rate, blood pressure, circulation, and digestion. Since you have more control over exhalations, focusing on this part of your breathing is one good way of learning how to breathe deeper. Use the muscles between your ribs to squeeze air out of your lungs—when you move more air out, you will automatically take more air in. As you breathe in and out, think of the cycle as having no beginning or end. Practice this exercise as often as you like, but I recommend doing it at least once each day."

Dr. Andrew Weil

The lungs should be allowed the greatest freedom possible. Their capacity is developed by free action; it diminishes if they are cramped and compressed. Hence the ill effects of the practice so common, especially in sedentary pursuits, of stooping at one's work. In this position it is impossible to breathe deeply. Superficial breathing soon becomes a habit, and the lungs lose their power to expand. (*Ministry of Healing*, page 272)

"A nation that destroys its soils destroys itself. Forests are the lungs of our land, purifying the air and giving fresh strength to our people."

Franklin Delano Roosevelt

Thus an insufficient supply of oxygen is received. The blood moves sluggishly. The waste, poisonous matter, which should be thrown off in the exhalations from the lungs, is retained, and the blood becomes impure. Not only the lungs, but the stomach, liver, and brain are affected. The skin becomes sallow, digestion is retarded; the heart is depressed; the brain is clouded; the thoughts are confused; gloom settles upon the spirits; the whole system becomes depressed and inactive, and peculiarly susceptible to disease. (*Ministry of Healing,* page 273)

> "Controlled deep breathing helps the body to transform the air we breathe into energy. The stream of energized air produced by properly executed and controlled deep breathing produces a current of inner energy which radiates throughout the entire body and can be channeled to the body areas that need it the most, on demand."
>
> Nancy Zi

In order to have good blood, we must breathe well. Full, deep inspirations of pure air, which fill the lungs with oxygen, purify the blood. They impart to it a bright color and send it, a life-giving current, to every part of the body. A good respiration soothes the nerves; it stimulates the appetite and renders digestion more perfect; and it induces sound, refreshing sleep. (*Ministry of Healing,* page 272)

> "Thank God men cannot fly, and lay waste the sky as well as the earth."
>
> Henry David Thoreau

In the construction of buildings, whether for public purposes or as dwellings, care should be taken to provide for good ventilation and plenty of sunlight. Churches and schoolrooms are often faulty in this respect. Neglect of proper ventilation is responsible for much of the drowsiness and dullness that destroy the effect of many a sermon and make the teacher's work toilsome and ineffective. (*Ministry of Healing,* page 274)

Food for Thought

"Inhale, and God approaches you. Hold the inhalation, and God remains with you. Exhale, and you approach God. Hold the exhalation, and surrender to God."

Sri Tirumalai Krishnamacharya

CARING FOR CHILDREN

Babies require warmth, but a serious error is often committed in keeping them in overheated rooms, deprived to a great degree of fresh air. The practice of covering the infant's face while sleeping is harmful, since it prevents free respiration. (*Ministry of Healing*, page 381)

> "Mothers and fathers have an unparalleled opportunity to help shape the personality of their unborn child. They can actively contribute to his happiness and well-being, and not just in utero, nor in the years immediately following birth, but for the rest of his life."
>
> Dr. Thomas Verny

Instead of sending her children from her, that she may not be annoyed by their noise or troubled by their little wants, let the mother plan amusement or light work to employ the active hands and minds. (*Ministry of Healing*, page 388)

> "The fear of failure is so great, it is no wonder that the desire to do right by one's children has led to a whole library of books offering advice on how to raise them."
>
> Bruno Bettelheim

Food for Thought

$\mathcal{P}$arents need to consider this. They should understand the principles that underlie the care and training of children. They should be capable of rearing them in physical, mental, and moral health. Parents should study the laws of nature. They should become acquainted with the organism of the human body. They need to understand the functions of the various organs, and their relation and dependence. They should study the relation of the mental to the physical powers, and the conditions required for the healthy action of each. To assume the responsibilities of parenthood without such preparation is a sin. (*Ministry of Healing,* page 380)

> "Parents can plant magic in a child's mind though certain words spoken with some thrilling quality of voice, some uplift of the heart and spirit."
>
> Robert MacNeil

In many cases the sickness of children can be traced to errors in management. Irregularities in eating, insufficient clothing in the chilly evening, lack of vigorous exercise to keep the blood in healthy circulation, or lack of abundance of air for its purification, may be the cause of the trouble. Let the parents study to find the causes of the sickness, and then remedy the wrong conditions as soon as possible. (*Ministry of Healing,* page 385)

> "You can do anything with children if you only play with them."
>
> Prince Otto von Bismarck

$\mathcal{B}$ut let not the children be neglected. Burdened with many cares, mothers sometimes feel that they cannot take time patiently to instruct their little ones and give them love and sympathy. But they should remember that if the children do

Food for Thought

not find in their parents and in their home that which will satisfy their desire for sympathy and companionship, they will look to other sources, where both mind and character may be endangered. (*Ministry of Healing*, page 389)

"What constitutes a child?—Want of instruction; for they are our equals so far as their degree of knowledge permits."

Epictetus

𝒫arents, let your children see that you love them and will do all in your power to make them happy. If you do so, your necessary restrictions will have far greater weight in their young minds. (*Ministry of Healing*, page 394)

"You don't really understand human nature unless you know why a child on a merry-go-round will wave at his parents every time around—and why his parents will always wave back."

William D. Tammeus

CARING FOR THE SICK

𝒯o a convalescent or a patient suffering from chronic disease, it is often a pleasure and a benefit to know that he is kindly remembered; but this assurance conveyed by a message of sympathy or by some little gift will often serve a better purpose than a personal visit, and without danger of harm. (*Ministry of Healing*, page 222)

Food for Thought

"The trained nurse has become one of the great blessings of humanity, taking a place beside the physician and the priest, and not inferior to either in her mission."

Sir William Osler

Exercise in the open air should be prescribed as a life-giving necessity. And for such exercises there is nothing better than the cultivation of the soil. Let patients have flower beds to care for, or work to do in the orchard or vegetable garden. As they are encouraged to leave their rooms and spend time in the open air, cultivating flowers or doing some other light, pleasant work, their attention will be diverted from themselves and their sufferings. (*Ministry of Healing*, page 265)

"Health is a state of complete harmony of the body, mind and spirit. When one is free from physical disabilities and mental distractions, the gates of the soul open."

B.K.S. Iyengar

In the treatment of the sick the effect of mental influence should not be overlooked. Rightly used, this influence affords one of the most effective agencies for combating disease. (*Ministry of Healing*, page 241)

"The poets did well to conjoin music and medicine in Apollo because the office of medicine is but to tune this curious harp of man's body and to reduce it to harmony."

Sir Francis Bacon

Those who minister to the sick should understand the importance of careful attention to the laws of health. (*Ministry of Healing*, page 219)

Food for Thought

"If I had my way I'd make health catching instead of disease."

Robert Ingersoll

Sympathy and tact will often prove a greater benefit to the sick than will the most skillful treatment given in a cold, indifferent way. When a physician comes to the sickbed with a listless, careless manner, looks at the afflicted one with little concern, by word or action giving the impression that the case is not one requiring much attention, and then leaves the patient to his own reflections, he has done that patient positive harm. The doubt and discouragement produced by his indifference will often counteract the good effect of the remedies he may prescribe. (*Ministry of Healing*, page 244)

"It's actually the spirit helping the spirit; it is the doctor, the bed, the potion."

Franz Grillparzer

It is misdirected kindness, a false idea of courtesy, that leads to much visiting of the sick. Those who are very ill should not have visitors. The excitement connected with receiving callers wearies the patient at a time when he is in the greatest need of quiet, undisturbed rest. (*Ministry of Healing*, page 222)

"Prevention is better than cure."

Desiderius Erasmus

CHARITY

Real charity helps men to help themselves. If one comes to our door and asks for food, we should not turn him away hungry; his poverty may be the result of misfortune. But true beneficence means more than mere gifts. It means a genuine interest in the welfare of others. We should seek to understand the needs of the poor and distressed, and to give them the help that will benefit them most. To give thought and time and personal effort costs far more than merely to give money. But it is the truest charity. (*Ministry of Healing,* page 195)

> "A bone to the dog is not charity. Charity is the bone shared with the dog, when you are just as hungry as the dog."
>
> Jack London

The journey made three times a year to the annual feasts at Jerusalem, the week's sojourn in booths during the Feast of Tabernacles, were opportunities for outdoor recreation and social life. These feasts were occasions of rejoicing, made sweeter and more tender by the hospitable welcome given to the stranger, the Levite, and the poor. (*Ministry of Healing,* page 281)

> "Time, which wears down and diminishes all things, augments and increases good deeds, because a good turn liberally offered to a reasonable man grows continually through noble thought and memory."
>
> François Rabelais

Unwise economy and artificial customs often prevent the exercise of hospitality where it is needed and would be a blessing. The regular supply of food for our tables should be such that the unexpected guest can be made welcome without burdening the housewife to make extra preparation. (*Ministry of Healing,* page 322)

"One cannot have too large a party."

Jane Austen

How can they be awakened to the necessity of improvement? How can they be directed to a higher ideal of life? How can they be helped to rise? What can be done where poverty prevails and is to be contended with at every step? Certainly the work is difficult. The necessary reformation will never be made unless men and women are assisted by a power outside of themselves. It is God's purpose that the rich and the poor shall be closely bound together by the ties of sympathy and helpfulness. Those who have means, talents, and capabilities are to use these gifts in blessing their fellow men. (*Ministry of Healing,* page 193)

"Virtue is its own reward. There's a pleasure in doing good which sufficiently pays itself."

Sir John Vanbrugh

If they ever become industrious and self-supporting, very many must have assistance, encouragement, and instruction. There are multitudes of poor families for whom no better missionary work could be done than to assist them in settling on the land and in learning how to make it yield them a livelihood. (*Ministry of Healing,* page 192)

"Poverty is the worst form of violence."

Mahatma Gandhi

The need for such help and instruction is not confined to the cities. Even in the country, with all its possibilities for a better life, multitudes of the poor are in great need. Whole communities are devoid of education in industrial and sanitary lines. Families live in hovels, with scant furniture and clothing, without tools, without books, destitute both of comforts and conveniences and of means of culture. Imbruted souls, bodies weak and ill-formed, reveal the results of evil heredity and of wrong habits. These people must be educated from the very foundation. They have led shiftless, idle, corrupt lives, and they need to be trained to correct habits. (*Ministry of Healing*, page 192)

> "How wonderful it is that nobody need wait a single moment before starting to improve the world."
>
> Anne Frank

CHILDREN'S DIETS

The importance of training children to right dietetic habits can hardly be overestimated. The little ones need to learn that they eat to live, not live to eat. The training should begin with the infant in its mother's arms. The child should be given food only at regular intervals, and less frequently as it grows older. It should not be given sweets, or the food of older persons, which it is unable to digest. Care and regularity in the feeding of infants will not only promote health, and thus tend to make them quiet and sweet-tempered, but will lay the foundation of habits that will be a blessing to them in after years. (*Ministry of Healing*, page 383)

Food for Thought

"Regularity of nursing is most important. The infant should always be fed exactly at the stated hour and never at irregular intervals, as this upsets the baby's routine and soon leads to stomach trouble. If the infant wakes up and cries before the feeding hour he should be examined to see if he is wet, and if so, changed and then offered some plain boiled water. If the infant is asleep at the feeding hour he should be awakened. It is remarkable how these infants learn to wake up at or shortly before the appointed time. After a few days."

Dr. Frederick Tisdall

The baby should be kept free from every influence that would tend to weaken or to poison the system. The most scrupulous care should be taken to have everything about it sweet and clean. (*Ministry of Healing*, page 381)

"I want to pass the word to parents that cow's milk has definite faults for some babies. It causes allergies, indigestion, and contributes to some cases of childhood diabetes."

Dr. Benjamin Spock

What the parents are, that, to a great extent, the children will be. The physical conditions of the parents, their dispositions and appetites, their mental and moral tendencies, are, to a greater or less degree, reproduced in their children. (*Ministry of Healing*, page 371)

"If our American way of life fails the child, it fails us all."

Pearl S. Buck

Food for Thought

CHILDREN'S NEEDS

The directions given concerning the Hebrew children teach us that nothing which affects the child's physical well-being is to be neglected. Nothing is unimportant. Every influence that affects the health of the body has its bearing upon mind and character. (*Ministry of Healing*, page 380)

> "I cannot think of any need in childhood as strong as the need for a father's protection."
>
> Sigmund Freud

Children have rights, they have preferences, and when these preferences are reasonable they should be respected. (*Ministry of Healing*, page 384)

> "If a child is to keep alive his inborn sense of wonder, he needs the companionship of at least one adult who can share it, rediscovering with him the joy, excitement and mystery of the world we live in."
>
> Rachel Carson

No barrier of coldness and reserve should be allowed to arise between parents and children. Let parents become acquainted with their children, seeking to understand their tastes and dispositions, entering into their feelings, and drawing out what is in their hearts. (*Ministry of Healing*, page 394)

> "Children will not remember you for the material things you provided but for the feeling that you cherished them."
>
> Richard L. Evans

Food for Thought

*B*etter than any other inheritance of wealth you can give to your children will be the gift of a healthy body, a sound mind, and a noble character. Those who understand what constitutes life's true success will be wise betimes. They will keep in view life's best things in their choice of a home. (*Ministry of Healing*, page 366)

> "You are worried about seeing him spend his early years in doing nothing. What! Is it nothing to be happy? Nothing to skip, play, and run around all day long? Never in his life will he be so busy again."
>
> Jean-Jacques Rousseau

CLEANLINESS

*I*t is important also that the clothing be kept clean. The garments worn absorb the waste matter that passes off through the pores; if they are not frequently changed and washed, the impurities will be reabsorbed. (*Ministry of Healing*, page 276)

> "Bath twice a day to be really clean, once a day to be passably clean, once a week to avoid being a public menace."
>
> Anthony Burgess

*N*ot only in their religious service, but in all the affairs of daily life was observed the distinction between clean and unclean. All who came in contact with contagious or contaminating diseases were isolated from the encampment, and they were not permitted to return without thorough cleansing of both the person and the clothing. (*Ministry of Healing*, page 277)

Food for Thought

"Cleanliness may be recommended as a mark of politeness, as it produces affection and as it bears analogy to purity of mind. As it renders us agreeable to others, so it makes us easy to ourselves. It is an excellent preservative of health; and several vices, destructive both to body and mind, are inconsistent with the habit of it."

Joseph Addison

Scrupulous cleanliness is essential to both physical and mental health. Impurities are constantly thrown off from the body through the skin. Its millions of pores are quickly clogged unless kept clean by frequent bathing, and the impurities which should pass off through the skin become an additional burden to the other eliminating organs. (*Ministry of Healing*, page 276)

"Certainly, this is a duty not a sin. Cleanliness is, indeed, next to Godliness."

John Wesley

Every form of uncleanliness tends to disease. Death-producing germs abound in dark, neglected corners, in decaying refuse, in dampness and mold and must. No waste vegetables or heaps of fallen leaves should be allowed to remain near the house to decay and poison the air. Nothing unclean or decaying should be tolerated within the home. In towns or cities regarded perfectly healthful, many an epidemic of fever has been traced to decaying matter about the dwelling of some careless householder. (*Ministry of Healing*, page 276)

"Cleanliness and order are not matters of instinct; they are matters of education, and like most great things—mathematics and classics—you must cultivate a taste for them."

Benjamin Disraeli

Food for Thought

*I*n the teaching that God gave to Israel, the preservation of health received careful attention. The people who had come from slavery with the uncleanly and unhealthful habits which it engenders, were subjected to the strictest training in the wilderness before entering Canaan. Health principles were taught and sanitary laws enforced.
(*Ministry of Healing,* page 277)

> "Throughout human history, the major problems of health that men have faced have been concerned with community life, for instance, the control of transmissible disease, the control and improvement of sanitation, the provision of water and food of good quality and in sufficient supply, the provision of medical care, and the relief of disability and destitution. The relative emphasis placed on each of these problems has varied from time to time, but they are all closely related, and from them has come public health as we know it today."
>
> George Rosen

*W*hen those who advocate hygienic reform go to extremes, it is no wonder that many who regard these persons as representing health principles reject the reform altogether. These extremes frequently do more harm in a short time than could be undone by a lifetime of consistent living.
(*Ministry of Healing,* page 324)

> "Respect for God demands that the face, the hands, and the feet be washed once a day."
>
> The Talmud

Food for Thought

COMFORT OF HOME

Home should be a place where cheerfulness, courtesy, and love abide; and where these graces dwell, there will abide happiness and peace. Troubles may invade, but these are the lot of humanity. Let patience, gratitude, and love keep sunshine in the heart, though the day may be ever so cloudy. In such homes angels of God abide. (*Ministry of Healing*, page 393)

> "The lust for comfort, that stealthy thing that enters the house as a guest, and then becomes a host, and then a master."
>
> Khalil Gibran

Nearly all dwellers in the country, however poor, could have about their homes a bit of grassy lawn, a few shade trees, flowering shrubbery, or fragrant blossoms. And far more than any artificial adorning will they minister to the happiness of the household. They will bring into the home life a softening, refining influence, strengthening the love of nature, and drawing the members of the household nearer to one another and nearer to God. (*Ministry of Healing*, page 370)

> " A letter from home is worth ten thousand ounces of gold."
>
> Chinese proverb

Above all things else, let parents surround their children with an atmosphere of cheerfulness, courtesy, and love. A home where love dwells, and where it is expressed in looks, in words, and in acts, is a place where angels delight to manifest their presence. (*Ministry of Healing*, page 386)

Food for Thought

"Home is a name, a word, it is a strong one; stronger than magician ever spoke, or spirit ever answered to, in the strongest conjuration."

Charles Dickens

The home should be to the children the most attractive place in the world, and the mother's presence should be its greatest attraction. Children have sensitive, loving natures. They are easily pleased and easily made unhappy. By gentle discipline, in loving words and acts, mothers may bind their children to their hearts. (*Ministry of Healing*, page 388)

"His house was perfect, whether you liked food, or sleep, or work, or storytelling, or singing, or just sitting and thinking, best, or a pleasant mixture of them all."

J.R.R. Tolkien

Our homes should be a place of refuge for the tempted youth. Many there are who stand at the parting of the ways. Every influence, every impression, is determining the choice that shapes their destiny both here and hereafter. Evil invites them. Its resorts are made bright and attractive. They have a welcome for every comer. All about us are youth who have no home, and many whose homes have no helpful, uplifting power, and the youth drift into evil. They are going down to ruin within the very shadow of our own doors. (*Ministry of Healing*, page 354)

"I had rather be on my farm than be emperor of the world."

George Washington

Food for Thought

COMPASSION FOR ANIMALS

The intelligence displayed by many dumb animals approaches so closely to human intelligence that it is a mystery. The animals see and hear and love and fear and suffer. They use their organs far more faithfully than many human beings use theirs. They manifest sympathy and tenderness toward their companions in suffering. Many animals show an affection for those who have charge of them, far superior to the affection shown by some of the human race. They form attachments for man which are not broken without great suffering to them. (*Ministry of Healing*, page 315)

> "I have from an early age abjured the use of meat, and the time will come when men such as I will look upon the murder of animals as they now look upon the murder of men."
>
> Leonardo da Vinci

Animals are often transported long distances and subjected to great suffering in reaching a market. Taken from the green pastures, and traveling for weary miles over the hot, dusty roads, or crowded into filthy cars, feverish and exhausted, often for many hours deprived of food and water, the poor creatures are driven to their death, that human beings may feast on the carcasses. (*Ministry of Healing*, page 314)

> "Animals are more than ever a test of our character, of mankind's capacity for empathy and for decent, honorable conduct and faithful stewardship . . . We are called to treat them with kindness, not because they have rights or power or some claim to equality, but in a sense because they don't; because they all stand unequal and powerless before us."
>
> Matthew Scully

Food for Thought

Often animals are taken to market and sold for food when they are so diseased that their owners fear to keep them longer. And some of the processes of fattening them for market produce disease. Shut away from the light and pure air, breathing the atmosphere of filthy stables, perhaps fattening on decaying food, the entire body soon becomes contaminated with foul matter. (*Ministry of Healing*, page 314)

> "The fate of animals is of greater importance to me than the fear of appearing ridiculous; it is indissolubly connected with the fate of men."
>
> — Émile Zola

The moral evils of a flesh diet are not less marked than are the physical ills. Flesh food is injurious to health, and whatever affects the body has a corresponding effect on the mind and the soul. Think of the cruelty to animals that meat eating involves, and its effect on those who inflict and those who behold it. How it destroys the tenderness with which we should regard these creatures of God! (*Ministry of Healing*, page 315)

> "The vegetarian movement ought to fill with gladness the souls of those who have at heart the realization of God's kingdom upon earth, not because vegetarianism itself is such an important step towards the realization of this kingdom, but because it serves as a criterion by which we know that the pursuit of moral perfection on the part of man is genuine and sincere."
>
> — Leo Tolstoy

Is it not time that all should aim to dispense with flesh foods? How can those who are seeking to become pure, refined, and holy, that they may have the companionship of heavenly angels, continue to use as food anything that has so harmful an effect on soul and body? How can they take the life of God's creatures that they may consume the flesh as a luxury? Let them, rather, return to the wholesome and delicious food given to man in the beginning, and themselves practice, and teach their children to practice, mercy toward the dumb creatures that God has made and has placed under our dominion. (*Ministry of Healing,* page 317)

> "We can judge the heart of a man by his treatment of animals."
>
> Immanuel Kant

What man with a human heart, who has ever cared for domestic animals, could look into their eyes, so full of confidence and affection, and willingly give them over to the butcher's knife? How could he devour their flesh as a sweet morsel? (*Ministry of Healing,* page 316)

> "Love animals: God has given them the rudiments of thought and joy untroubled. Do not trouble their joy, do not harass them, do not deprive them of their happiness, do not work against God's intent. Man, do not pride yourself upon your superiority to animals: they are without sin, and you, with your greatness, defile the earth by your appearance on it, and leave the traces of your foulness after you."
>
> Fyodor Dostoevsky

Food for Thought

COMPASSION FOR OTHERS

We can do nothing without courage and perseverance. Speak words of hope and courage to the poor and the disheartened. If need be, give tangible proof of your interest by helping them when they come into strait places. Those who have had many advantages should remember that they themselves still err in many things, and that it is painful to them when their errors are pointed out and there is held up before them a comely pattern of what they should be. Remember that kindness will accomplish more than censure. As you try to teach others, let them see that you wish them to reach the highest standard, and that you are ready to give them help. If in some things they fail, be not quick to condemn them. (*Ministry of Healing*, page 196)

> "One should never direct people towards happiness, because happiness too is an idol of the marketplace. One should direct them towards mutual affection. A beast gnawing at its prey can be happy too, but only human beings can feel affection for each other, and this is the highest achievement they can aspire to."
>
> Aleksandr Solzhenitsyn

Every association of life calls for the exercise of self-control, forbearance, and sympathy. We differ so widely in disposition, habits, education, that our ways of looking at things vary. We judge differently. Our understanding of truth, our ideas in regard to the conduct of life, are not in all respects the same. There are no two whose experience is alike in every particular. The trials of one are not the trials of another. The duties that one finds light are to another most difficult and perplexing. (*Ministry of Healing*, page 483)

Food for Thought

> "Your cultivation of love and great compassion should not be left in a state of mere imagination or wish alone; rather, a sense of responsibility, a genuine intention to engage in the task of relieving sentient beings of their sufferings and providing them with happiness, should be developed."
>
> Tenzin Gyatso, Dalai Lama

When all has been done that can be done in helping the poor to help themselves, there still remain the widow and the fatherless, the aged, the helpless, and the sick, that claim sympathy and care. (*Ministry of Healing*, page 201)

> "Becoming responsible adults is no longer a matter of whether children hang up their pajamas or put dirty towels in the hamper, but whether they care about themselves and others—and whether they see everyday chores as related to how we treat this planet."
>
> Eda LeShan

Men and women have hardly begun to understand the true object of life. They are attracted by glitter and show. They are ambitious for worldly pre-eminence. To this the true aims of life are sacrificed. Life's best things—simplicity, honesty, truthfulness, purity, integrity—cannot be bought or sold. They are as free to the ignorant as to the educated, to the humble laborer as to the honored statesman. For everyone God has provided pleasure that may be enjoyed by rich and poor alike—the pleasure found in cultivating pureness of thought and unselfishness of action, the pleasure that comes from speaking sympathizing words and doing kindly deeds. From those who perform such service the light of Christ shines to brighten lives darkened by many shadows. (*Ministry of Healing*, page 198)

Food for Thought

"How far you go in life depends on your being tender with the young, compassionate with the aged, sympathetic with the striving, and tolerant of the weak and the strong. Because someday in your life, you will have been all of these."

George Washington Carver

As the members of a true family care for one another, ministering to the sick, supporting the weak, teaching the ignorant, training the inexperienced, so is "the household of faith" to care for its needy and helpless ones. Upon no consideration are these to be passed by. (*Ministry of Healing*, page 201)

"If you haven't any charity in your heart, you have the worst kind of heart trouble."

Bob Hope

If physicians could put themselves in the place of the one whose spirit is humbled and whose will is weakened by suffering, and who longs for words of sympathy and assurance, they would be better prepared to appreciate his feelings. When the love and sympathy that Christ manifested for the sick is combined with the physician's knowledge, his very presence will be a blessing. (*Ministry of Healing*, page 245)

"Service to others is the rent you pay for your room here on earth."

Muhammad Ali

In sanitariums and hospitals, where nurses are constantly associated with large numbers of sick people, it requires a decided effort to be always pleasant and cheerful, and to show thoughtful consideration in every word and act. (*Ministry of Healing*, page 222)

Food for Thought

> "Grace is nothing else but a certain beginning of glory in us."
>
> St. Thomas Aquinas

Not all the poor in the city slums are of this class. God-fearing men and women have been brought to the depths of poverty by illness or misfortune, often through the dishonest scheming of those who live by preying upon their fellows. Many who are upright and well-meaning become poor through lack of industrial training. Through ignorance they are unfitted to wrestle with the difficulties of life. Drifting into the cities, they are often unable to find employment. Surrounded by the sights and sounds of vice, they are subjected to terrible temptation. Herded and often classed with the vicious and degraded, it is only by a superhuman struggle, a more than finite power, that they can be preserved from sinking to the same depths. Many hold fast their integrity, choosing to suffer rather than to sin. This class especially demand help, sympathy, and encouragement. (*Ministry of Healing,* page 190)

> "The capacity to give one's attention to a sufferer is a very rare and difficult thing; it is almost a miracle; it is a miracle. Nearly all those who think they have this capacity do not possess it. Warmth of heart, impulsiveness, pity are not enough."
>
> Simone Weil

Food for Thought

COOKING HEALTHY FOOD

When properly prepared, olives, like nuts, supply the place of butter and flesh meats. The oil, as eaten in the olive, is far preferable to animal oil or fat. It serves as a laxative. Its use will be found beneficial to consumptives, and it is healing to an inflamed, irritated stomach. (*Ministry of Healing*, page 298)

> "The secret of a live, clean body is live, clean food—fresh vegetables, juices, fruit, and nice green salads. As long as people continue to eat foods that have been prepared of impoverished, ghostly white flour, bleached and sulphured foods, doped and adulterated foods, plaster-like preparations called breakfast cereals; so long as they live on inferior food, material that has been dyed, chemically treated, doctored up so that it will look and feel fresh far past the time when it should have spoiled; that long will they continue to be half alive and sick."
>
> Lester Roloff

Scanty, ill-cooked food depraves the blood by weakening the blood-making organs. It deranges the system and brings on disease, with its accompaniment of irritable nerves and bad tempers. The victims of poor cookery are numbered by thousands and tens of thousands. Over many graves might be written: "Died because of poor cooking;" "Died of an abused stomach." (*Ministry of Healing*, page 302)

> "There are only ten minutes in the life of a pear when it is perfect to eat."
>
> Ralph Waldo Emerson

Food for Thought

The diet reform should be progressive. As disease in animals increases, the use of milk and eggs will become more and more unsafe. An effort should be made to supply their place with other things that are healthful and inexpensive. The people everywhere should be taught how to cook without milk and eggs, so far as possible, and yet have their food wholesome and palatable. (*Ministry of Healing*, page 320)

> "Life expectancy would grow by leaps and bounds if green vegetables smelled as good as bacon."
>
> Doug Larson

COOKING INSTRUCTIONS

Every woman who is at the head of a family and yet does not understand the art of healthful cookery should determine to learn that which is so essential to the well-being of her household. In many places hygienic cooking schools afford opportunity for instruction in this line. She who has not the help of such facilities should put herself under the instruction of some good cook and persevere in her efforts for improvement until she is mistress of the culinary art. (*Ministry of Healing*, page 303)

> "The fact is that it takes more than ingredients and technique to cook a good meal. A good cook puts something of himself into the preparation—he cooks with enjoyment, anticipation, spontaneity, and he is willing to experiment."
>
> Pearl Bailey

Food for Thought

The meals should be varied. The same dishes, prepared in the same way, should not appear on the table meal after meal and day after day. The meals are eaten with greater relish, and the system is better nourished, when the food is varied. (*Ministry of Healing*, page 300)

> "The secret of good cooking is, first, having a love of it. If you're convinced that cooking is drudgery, you're never going to be good at it, and you might as well warm up something frozen."
>
> James Beard

It is a sacred duty for those who cook to learn how to prepare healthful food. Many souls are lost as the result of poor cookery. It takes thought and care to make good bread; but there is more religion in a loaf of good bread than many think. There are few really good cooks. Young women think that it is menial to cook and do other kinds of housework, and for this reason many girls who marry and have the care of families have little idea of the duties devolving upon a wife and mother. (*Ministry of Healing*, page 302)

> "In order to make an apple pie from scratch, you must first create the universe."
>
> Carl Sagan

All should learn what to eat and how to cook it. Men, as well as women, need to understand the simple, healthful preparation of food. Their business often calls them where they cannot obtain wholesome food; then, if they have a knowledge of cookery, they can use it to good purpose. (*Ministry of Healing*, page 323)

Food for Thought

> "To the old saying that man built the house but woman made of it a home might be added the modern supplement that woman accepted cooking as a chore but man has made of it a recreation."
>
> Emily Post

Cooking is no mean science, and it is one of the most essential in practical life. It is a science that all women should learn, and it should be taught in a way to benefit the poorer classes. To make food appetizing and at the same time simple and nourishing, requires skill; but it can be done. Cooks should know how to prepare simple food in a simple and healthful manner, and so that it will be found more palatable, as well as more wholesome, because of its simplicity. (*Ministry of Healing*, page 302)

> "Give us this day our daily taste. Restore to us soups that spoons will not sink in and sauces which are never the same twice. Raise up among us stews with more gravy than we have bread to blot it with . . . Give us pasta with a hundred fillings."
>
> Robert Farrar Capon

COUNTRY LIVING

If the poor now crowded into the cities could find homes upon the land, they might not only earn a livelihood, but find health and happiness now unknown to them. Hard work, simple fare, close economy, often hardship and privation, would be their lot. But what a blessing would be theirs in leaving the city, with its enticements to evil, its turmoil and crime, misery and foulness, for the country's quiet and peace and purity. (*Ministry of Healing*, page 190)

Food for Thought

"I said to myself—I'll paint what I see—what the flower is to me but I'll paint it big and they will be surprised into taking time to look at it—I will make even busy New Yorkers take time to see what I see of flowers."

Georgia O'Keeffe

Instead of dwelling where only the works of men can be seen, where the sights and sounds frequently suggest thoughts of evil, where turmoil and confusion bring weariness and disquietude, go where you can look upon the works of God. Find rest of spirit in the beauty and quietude and peace of nature. Let the eye rest on the green fields, the groves, and the hills. Look up to the blue sky, unobscured by the city's dust and smoke, and breathe the invigorating air of heaven. Go where, apart from the distractions and dissipations of city life, you can give your children your companionship, where you can teach them to learn of God through His works, and train them for lives of integrity and usefulness. (*Ministry of Healing*, page 367)

"Our rural village life was a purifying, uplifting influence."

Agnes E. Meyer

To many of those living in the cities who have not a spot of green grass to set their feet upon, who year after year have looked out upon filthy courts and narrow alleys, brick walls and pavements, and skies clouded with dust and smoke—if these could be taken to some farming district, surrounded with the green fields, the woods and hills and brooks, the clear skies and the fresh, pure air of the country, it would seem almost like heaven. (*Ministry of Healing*, page 191)

> "The air and the earth interpenetrated in the warm gusts of spring; the soil was full of sunlight, and the sunlight full of red dust. The air one breathed was saturated with earthy smells, and the grass under foot had a reflection of the blue sky in it."
>
> Willa Cather

And for those who are weak in moral power, the cities abound in dangers. In them, patients who have unnatural appetites to overcome are continually exposed to temptation. They need to be placed amid new surroundings where the current of their thoughts will be changed; they need to be placed under influences wholly different from those that have wrecked their lives. Let them for a season be removed from those influences that lead away from God, into a purer atmosphere. (*Ministry of Healing,* page 263)

> "There is nothing like walking to get the feel of a country. A fine landscape is like a piece of music; it must be taken at the right tempo. Even a bicycle goes too fast."
>
> Paul Scott Mowrer

DETERMINATION

Because they have not the determination to take themselves in hand and to reform, many become stereotyped in a wrong course of action. But this need not be. They may cultivate their powers to do the very best kind of service, and then they will be always in demand. They will be valued for all that they are worth. (*Ministry of Healing,* page 477)

Food for Thought

"It is a blessed thing that in every age someone has had the individuality enough and courage enough to stand by his own convictions."

Robert G. Ingersoll

Forbearance and unselfishness mark the words and acts of all who live the new life in Christ. As you seek to live His life, striving to conquer self and selfishness and to minister to the needs of others, you will gain victory after victory. Thus your influence will bless the world. (*Ministry of Healing,* page 362)

"Formulate and stamp indelibly on your mind a mental picture of yourself as succeeding. Hold this picture tenaciously. Never permit it to fade. Your mind will seek to develop the picture . . . Do not build up obstacles in your imagination."

Norman Vincent Peale

Those who are taught to earn what they receive will more readily learn to make the most of it. And in learning to be self-reliant, they are acquiring that which will not only make them self-sustaining, but will enable them to help others. Teach the importance of life's duties to those who are wasting their opportunities. (*Ministry of Healing,* page 195)

"The mind is the limit. As long as the mind can envision the fact that you can do something, you can do it— as long as you really believe 100 percent."

Arnold Schwarzenegger

DIET AND EXERCISE

Exercise aids the dyspeptic by giving the digestive organs a healthy tone. To engage in severe study or violent physical exercise immediately after eating, hinders the work of digestion; but a short walk after a meal, with the head erect and the shoulders back, is a great benefit. (*Ministry of Healing*, page 240)

> "So you wish to conquer in the Olympic games, my friend? And I too, by the Gods, and a fine thing it would be! But first mark the conditions and the consequences, and then set to work. You will have to put yourself under discipline; to eat by rule, to avoid cakes and sweetmeats; to take exercise at the appointed hour whether you like it or no, in cold and heat; to abstain from cold drinks and from wine."
>
> Epictetus

Many writers and speakers fail here. After eating heartily, they give themselves to sedentary occupations, reading, study, or writing, allowing no time for physical exercise. As a consequence the free flow of thought and words is checked. They cannot write or speak with the force and intensity necessary in order to reach the heart; their efforts are tame and fruitless. (*Ministry of Healing*, page 309)

> "Everyone should be his own physician. We ought to assist and not force nature. Eat with moderation and with what agrees with your constitution. Nothing is good for the body but what we can digest. What medicine can produce digestion? Exercise. What will recruit strength? Sleep. What will alleviate incurable ills? Patience."
>
> Voltaire

Food for Thought

Strong men who are engaged in active physical labor are not compelled to be as careful as to the quantity or quality of their food as are persons of sedentary habits; but even these would have better health if they would practice self-control in eating and drinking. (*Ministry of Healing*, page 310)

> "If we could give every individual the right amount of nourishment and exercise, not too little and not too much, we would have found the safest way to health."
>
> Hippocrates

Notwithstanding all that is said and written concerning its importance, there are still many who neglect physical exercise. Some grow corpulent because the system is clogged; others become thin and feeble because their vital powers are exhausted in disposing of an excess of food. The liver is burdened in its effort to cleanse the blood of impurities, and illness is the result. (*Ministry of Healing*, page 240)

> "When it comes to eating right and exercising, there is no 'I'll start tomorrow.' Tomorrow is disease."
>
> V.L. Allineare

Here is a suggestion for all whose work is sedentary or chiefly mental; let those who have sufficient moral courage and self-control try it: At each meal take only two or three kinds of simple food, and eat no more than is required to satisfy hunger. Take active exercise every day, and see if you do not receive benefit. (*Ministry of Healing*, page 310)

> "Those who think they have not time for bodily exercise will sooner or later have to find time for illness."
>
> Edward Stanley

Food for Thought

DIETING RULES

Food should not be eaten very hot or very cold. If food is cold, the vital force of the stomach is drawn upon in order to warm it before digestion can take place. Cold drinks are injurious for the same reason; while the free use of hot drinks is debilitating. In fact, the more liquid there is taken with the meals, the more difficult it is for the food to digest; for the liquid must be absorbed before digestion can begin. Do not eat largely of salt, avoid the use of pickles and spiced foods, eat an abundance of fruit, and the irritation that calls for so much drink at mealtime will largely disappear. (*Ministry of Healing,* page 305)

> "The two biggest sellers in bookstores are the cookbooks and the diet books. The cookbooks tell you how to prepare the food and the diet books tell you how not to eat any of it."
>
> Andy Rooney

Custom has decreed that the food shall be placed upon the table in courses. Not knowing what is coming next, one may eat a sufficiency of food which perhaps is not the best suited to him. When the last course is brought on, he often ventures to overstep the bounds, and take the tempting dessert, which, however, proves anything but good for him. If all the food intended for a meal is placed on the table at the beginning, one has opportunity to make the best choice. (*Ministry of Healing,* page 306)

> "I am convinced that a light supper, a good night's sleep, and a fine morning, have sometimes made a hero of the same man, who, by an indigestion, a restless night, and rainy morning, would have proved a coward."
>
> Philip Dormer Stanhope, Fourth Earl of Chesterfield

Food for Thought

*I*n many cases the faintness that leads to a desire for food is felt because the digestive organs have been too severely taxed during the day. After disposing of one meal, the digestive organs need rest. At least five or six hours should intervene between the meals, and most persons who give the plan a trial will find that two meals a day are better than three. (*Ministry of Healing,* page 304)

> "Fruit should never be eaten with or immediately following anything. It is essential that when you eat fruit, it is eaten on an empty stomach. Fruit is the most important food you can eat. But if fruit is eaten on top of other foods, many problems result."
>
> Harvey Diamond

*R*egularity in eating should be carefully observed. Nothing should be eaten between meals, no confectionery, nuts, fruits, or food of any kind. Irregularities in eating destroy the healthful tone of the digestive organs, to the detriment of health and cheerfulness. And when the children come to the table, they do not relish wholesome food; their appetites crave that which is hurtful for them. (*Ministry of Healing,* page 384)

> "Appetite is essentially insatiable, and where it operates as a criterion of both action and enjoyment (that is, everywhere in the Western world since the sixteenth century) it will infallibly discover congenial agencies (mechanical and political) of expression."
>
> Marshall McLuhan

*B*ut not all foods wholesome in themselves are equally suited to our needs under all circumstances. Care should be taken in the selection of food. Our diet should be suited to the season, to the climate in which we live, and to the occupation we follow. Some foods that are adapted for use at one season or in one climate are not suited to another. So there are different foods best suited for

Food for Thought

persons in different occupations. Often food that can be used with benefit by those engaged in hard physical labor is unsuitable for persons of sedentary pursuits or intense mental application. God has given us ample variety of healthful foods, and each person should choose from it the things that experience and sound judgment prove to be best suited to his own necessities. (*Ministry of Healing*, page 296)

> "There are sound physiological reasons for eating foods in compatible combinations. In other words, some foods, if mixed in the digestive system, will cause distress! The principles of food combining are dictated by digestive chemistry. Different foods are digested differently. Starchy foods require an alkaline digestive medium which is supplied initially in the mouth by the enzyme ptyalin. Protein foods require an acid medium for digestion—hydrochloric acid."
>
> Dr. Herbert Shelton

Grains used for porridge or "mush" should have several hours cooking. But soft or liquid foods are less wholesome than dry foods, which require thorough mastication. Zwieback, or twice-baked bread, is one of the most easily digested and most palatable of foods. Let ordinary raised bread be cut in slices and dried in a warm oven till the last trace of moisture disappears. Then let it be browned slightly all the way through. In a dry place this bread can be kept much longer than ordinary bread, and, if reheated before using, it will be as fresh as when new. (*Ministry of Healing*, page 301)

> "Even matter called inorganic, believed to be dead, responds to irritants and gives unmistakable evidence of a living principle within. Everything that exists, organic or inorganic, animated or inert, is susceptible to stimulus from the outside."
>
> Nikola Tesla

Food for Thought

Food should be eaten slowly and should be thoroughly masticated. This is necessary in order that the saliva may be properly mixed with the food and the digestive fluids be called into action. (*Ministry of Healing*, page 305)

> "There is no plant which bears a fruit of as great importance as the olive."
>
> Pliny

Carefully consider your diet. Study from cause to effect. Cultivate self-control. Keep appetite under the control of reason. Never abuse the stomach by overeating, but do not deprive yourself of the wholesome, palatable food that health demands. (*Ministry of Healing*, page 323)

> "A man's palate can, in time, become accustomed to anything."
>
> Napoléon Bonaparte

Regularity in eating is of vital importance. There should be a specified time for each meal. At this time let everyone eat what the system requires and then take nothing more until the next meal. There are many who eat when the system needs no food, at irregular intervals, and between meals, because they have not sufficient strength of will to resist inclination. When traveling, some are constantly nibbling if anything eatable is within their reach. This is very injurious. If travelers would eat regularly of food that is simple and nutritious, they would not feel so great weariness nor suffer so much from sickness. (*Ministry of Healing*, page 303)

Food for Thought

"It is my view that the vegetarian manner of living by its purely physical effect on the human temperament would most beneficially influence the lot of mankind."

Albert Einstein

Persons who have accustomed themselves to a rich, highly stimulating diet have an unnatural taste, and they cannot at once relish food that is plain and simple. It will take time for the taste to become natural and for the stomach to recover from the abuse it has suffered. But those who persevere in the use of wholesome food will, after a time, find it palatable. Its delicate and delicious flavors will be appreciated, and it will be eaten with greater enjoyment than can be derived from unwholesome dainties. And the stomach, in a healthy condition, neither fevered nor overtaxed, can readily perform its task. (*Ministry of Healing*, page 298)

"Animals feed; man eats; only a man of wit knows how to eat."

Jean Anthelme Brillat-Savarin

Another serious evil is eating at improper times, as after violent or excessive exercise, when one is much exhausted or heated. Immediately after eating there is a strong draft upon the nervous energies; and when mind or body is heavily taxed just before or just after eating, digestion is hindered. When one is excited, anxious, or hurried, it is better not to eat until rest or relief is found. (*Ministry of Healing*, page 305)

"Don't dig your grave with your own knife and fork."

English proverb

Food for Thought

DISEASES

𝒫eople are continually eating flesh that is filled with tuberculosis and cancerous germs. Tuberculosis, cancer, and other fatal diseases are thus communicated. (*Ministry of Healing*, page 313)

> "Madness is locked beneath. It goes into tissues, is swallowed by the cells. The cells go mad. Cancer is their flag. Cancer is the growth of madness denied."
>
> Norman Mailer

𝐼f proper precaution is observed, non-contagious diseases need not be taken by others. Let the habits be correct, and by cleanliness and proper ventilation keep the sickroom free from poisonous elements. Under such conditions, the sick are much more likely to recover, and in most cases neither attendants nor the members of the family will contract the disease. (*Ministry of Healing*, page 220)

> "Disease is the retribution of outraged Nature."
>
> Hosea Ballou

𝒲hen a physician sees a patient suffering from disease caused by improper eating and drinking or other wrong habits, yet neglects to tell him of this, he is doing his fellow being an injury. Those who understand the principles of life should be in earnest in striving to counteract the causes of disease. Seeing the continual conflict with pain, laboring constantly to alleviate suffering, how can the physician hold his peace? (*Ministry of Healing*, page 114)

Food for Thought

> "Thousand upon thousands of persons have studied disease. Almost no one has studied health."
>
> — Adelle Davis

Disease never comes without a cause. The way is prepared, and disease invited, by disregard of the laws of health. Many suffer in consequence of the transgression of their parents. While they are not responsible for what their parents have done, it is nevertheless their duty to ascertain what are and what are not violations of the laws of health. They should avoid the wrong habits of their parents and, by correct living, place themselves in better conditions. (*Ministry of Healing*, page 234)

> "Everyone should know that most cancer research is largely a fraud, and that the major cancer research organizations are derelict in their duties to the people who support them."
>
> — Linus Pauling

Education in health principles was never more needed than now. Notwithstanding the wonderful progress in so many lines relating to the comforts and conveniences of life, even to sanitary matters and to the treatment of disease, the decline in physical vigor and power of endurance is alarming. It demands the attention of all who have at heart the well-being of their fellow men. (*Ministry of Healing*, page 125)

> "Cancer, above all other diseases, has countless secondary causes, but there is only one prime cause. The prime cause of cancer is the replacement of the normal oxygen respiration of body cells by an anaerobic cell respiration."
>
> — Dr. Otto Warburg

Food for Thought

The constant liability to contact with disease, the prevalence of foul air, impure water, impure food, the crowded, dark, unhealthful dwellings, are some of the many evils to be met. (*Ministry of Healing,* page 365)

> "It is more important to know what sort of person has a disease than to know what sort of disease a person has."
>
> — Hippocrates

When the abuse of health is carried so far that sickness results, the sufferer can often do for himself what no one else can do for him. The first thing to be done is to ascertain the true character of the sickness and then go to work intelligently to remove the cause. If the harmonious working of the system has become unbalanced by overwork, overeating, or other irregularities, do not endeavor to adjust the difficulties by adding a burden of poisonous medicines. (*Ministry of Healing,* page 235)

> "We have met the enemy and he is us."
>
> — Pogo Possum

DOCTORS

The physician who ministers in the homes of the people, watching at the bedside of the sick, relieving their distress, bringing them back from the borders of the grave, speaking hope to the dying, wins a place in their confidence and affection, such as is granted to few others. Not even to the minister of the gospel are committed possibilities so great or an influence so far-reaching. (*Ministry of Healing*, page 132)

> "The physician must not only be the healer, but often the counselor."
>
> Dr. Harriot K. Hunt

Every physician should realize that he who does weak, inefficient work is not only doing injury to the sick, but is also doing injustice to his fellow physicians. The physician who is satisfied with a low standard of skill and knowledge not only belittles the medical profession, but does dishonor to Christ, the Chief Physician. (*Ministry of Healing*, page 116)

> "He's the best physician that knows the worthlessness of the most medicines."
>
> Benjamin Franklin

The duties of the physician are arduous and trying. In order to perform them most successfully he needs to have a strong constitution and vigorous health. A man that is feeble or diseased cannot endure the wearing labor incident to the physician's calling. One who lacks perfect self-control cannot become qualified to deal with all classes of disease. (*Ministry of Healing*, page 135)

> "He who cures a disease may be the skillfullest, but he that prevents it is the safest physician."
>
> Thomas Fuller

Food for Thought

Frankness in dealing with a patient inspires him with confidence, and thus proves an important aid to recovery. There are physicians who consider it wise policy to conceal from the patient the nature and cause of the disease from which he is suffering. Many, fearing to excite or discourage a patient by stating the truth, will hold out false hopes of recovery, and even allow a patient to go down to the grave without warning him of his danger. All this is unwise. It may not always be safe or best to explain to the patient the full extent of his danger. This might alarm him and retard or even prevent recovery. Nor can the whole truth always be told to those whose ailments are largely imaginary. Many of these persons are unreasonable, and have not accustomed themselves to exercise self-control. They have peculiar fancies, and imagine many things that are false in regard to themselves and to others. To them these things are real, and those who care for them need to manifest constant kindness and unwearied patience and tact. But though the truth may not all be spoken on all occasions, it is never necessary or justifiable to deceive. Never should the physician or the nurse stoop to prevarication. He who does this places himself where God cannot cooperate with him, and in forfeiting the confidence of his patients he is casting away one of the most effective human aids to their restoration. (*Ministry of Healing*, page 245)

> "A man who cannot work without his hypodermic needle is a poor doctor. The amount of narcotic you use is inversely proportional to your skill."
>
> Dr. Martin H. Fischer

EATING POORLY

Those foods should be chosen that best supply the elements needed for building up the body. In this choice, appetite is not a safe guide. Through wrong habits of eating, the appetite has become perverted. Often it demands food that impairs health and causes weakness instead of strength. We cannot safely be guided by the customs of society. The disease and suffering that everywhere prevail are largely due to popular errors in regard to diet. (*Ministry of Healing,* page 295)

> "Indigestion is charged by God with enforcing morality on the stomach."
>
> Victor Hugo

Because principle requires us to discard those things that irritate the stomach and impair health, we should remember that an impoverished diet produces poverty of the blood. Cases of disease most difficult to cure result from this cause. The system is not sufficiently nourished, and dyspepsia and general debility are the result. Those who use such a diet are not always compelled by poverty to do so, but they choose it through ignorance or negligence, or to carry out their erroneous ideas of reform. (*Ministry of Healing,* page 321)

> "Americans will eat garbage provided you sprinkle it liberally with ketchup."
>
> Henry Miller

The stomach is closely related to the brain; and when the stomach diseased, the nerve power is called from the brain to the aid of the weakened digestive organs. When these demands are too frequent, the brain becomes congested. When the brain is constantly taxed, and there is lack of physical exercise, even plain food should be eaten sparingly. At mealtime cast off care and anxious thought; do not feel hurried, but eat slowly and with cheerfulness, with your heart filled with gratitude to God for all His blessings. (*Ministry of Healing,* page 306)

> "Men dig their graves with their own teeth and die more by those fated instruments than by the weapons of their enemies."
>
> Thomas Moffet

Because of these results, many suppose that their tea or coffee is doing them great good. But this is a mistake. Tea and coffee do not nourish the system. Their effect is produced before there has been time for digestion and assimilation, and what seems to be strength is only nervous excitement. When the influence of the stimulant is gone, the unnatural force abates, and the result is a corresponding degree of languor and debility. (*Ministry of Healing,* page 326)

> "Intemperance is naturally punished with diseases; rashness, with mischance; injustice, with violence of enemies; pride, with ruin; cowardice, with oppression; and rebellion, with slaughter."
>
> Thomas Hobbes

In relation to tea, coffee, tobacco, and alcoholic drinks, the only safe course is to touch not, taste not, handle not. The tendency of tea, coffee, and similar drinks is in the same direction as that of alcoholic liquor and tobacco, and in some cases the habit is as difficult to break as it is for the drunkard to give up intoxicants. Those who attempt to leave off these stimulants will for a time feel a loss and will suffer without them. But by persistence they will overcome the craving and cease to feel the lack. Nature may require a little time to recover from the abuse she has suffered; but give her a chance, and she will again rally and perform her work nobly and well. (*Ministry of Healing*, page 335)

> "Sugar will contribute to obesity, elevated triglycerides and cholesterol, and rot your teeth."
>
> Dr. John McDougall

Where wrong habits of diet have been indulged, there should be no delay in reform. When dyspepsia has resulted from abuse of the stomach, efforts should be made carefully to preserve the remaining strength of the vital forces by removing every overtaxing burden. The stomach may never entirely recover health after long abuse; but a proper course of diet will save further debility, and many will recover more or less fully. It is not easy to prescribe rules that will meet every case; but, with attention to right principles in eating, great reforms may be made, and the cook need not be continually toiling to tempt the appetite. (*Ministry of Healing*, page 308)

> "Lack of water in the body—chronic dehydration—is the root cause of many painful degenerative diseases, asthma, allergies, hypertension, excess body weight, and some emotional problems including depression."
>
> Dr. Fereydoon Batmanghelidj

Intemperate eating is often the cause of sickness, and what nature most needs is to be relieved of the undue burden that has been placed upon her. In many cases of sickness, the very best remedy is for the patient to fast for a meal or two, that the overworked organs of digestion may have an opportunity to rest. A fruit diet for a few days has often brought great relief to brain

Food for Thought

workers. Many times a short period of entire abstinence from food, followed by simple, moderate eating, has led to recovery through nature's own recuperative effort. An abstemious diet for a month or two would convince many sufferers that the path of self-denial is the path to health. (*Ministry of Healing*, page 235)

> "Everything I eat has been proved by some doctor or other to be a deadly poison, and everything I don't eat has been proved to be indispensable for life. But I go marching on."
>
> George Bernard Shaw

Another class, in their desire to set a right example, go to the opposite extreme. Some are unable to obtain the most desirable foods, and, instead of using such things as would best supply the lack, they adopt an impoverished diet. Their food does not supply the elements needed to make good blood. Their health suffers, their usefulness is impaired, and their example tells against, rather than in favor of, reform in diet. (*Ministry of Healing*, page 318)

> "In general, mankind, since the improvement in cookery, eats twice as much as nature requires."
>
> Benjamin Franklin

Sometimes the result of overeating is felt at once. In other cases there is no sensation of pain; but the digestive organs lose their vital force, and the foundation of physical strength is undermined. (*Ministry of Healing*, page 306)

> "Eating too much meat gives you indigestion and evil thoughts make you eat too much meat."
>
> Gertrude Stein

*E*very day men in positions of trust have decisions to make upon which depend results of great importance. Often they have to think rapidly, and this can be done successfully by those only who practice strict temperance. The mind strengthens under the correct treatment of the physical and mental powers. If the strain is not too great, new vigor comes with every taxation. But often the work of those who have important plans to consider and important decisions to make is affected for evil by the results of improper diet. A disordered stomach produces a disordered, uncertain state of mind. Often it causes irritability, harshness, or injustice. Many a plan that would have been a blessing to the world has been set aside, many unjust, oppressive, even cruel measures have been carried, as the result of diseased conditions due to wrong habits of eating. (*Ministry of Healing,* page 309)

> "Tell me what you eat and I'll tell you who you are."
>
> Jean Anthelme Brillat-Savarin

EATING PROPERLY

*T*here is real common sense in dietetic reform. The subject should be studied broadly and deeply, and no one should criticize others because their practice is not, in all things, in harmony with his own. It is impossible to make an unvarying rule to regulate everyone's habits, and no one should think himself a criterion for all. Not all can eat the same things. Foods that are palatable and wholesome to one person may be distasteful, and even harmful, to another. Some cannot use milk, while others thrive on it. Some persons cannot digest peas and beans; others find them wholesome. For some the coarser grain preparations are good food, while others cannot use them. (*Ministry of Healing,* page 319)

> "To eat is a necessity, but to eat intelligently is an art."
>
> François de La Rochefoucauld

The narrow ideas of some would-be health reformers have been a great injury to the cause of hygiene. Hygienists should remember that dietetic reform will be judged, to a great degree, by the provision they make for their tables; and instead of taking a course that will bring discredit upon it, they should so exemplify its principles as to commend them to candid minds. They consult taste instead of reason or the laws of health. (*Ministry of Healing,* page 323)

> "Nature will castigate those who don't masticate."
>
> Horace

Others think that since health requires a simple diet, there need be little care in the selection or the preparation of food. Some restrict themselves to a very meager diet, not having sufficient variety to supply the needs of the system, and they suffer in consequence. (*Ministry of Healing,* page 318)

> "Some people have a foolish way of not minding, or pretending not to mind, what they eat. For my part, I mind my belly very studiously, and very carefully; for I look upon it, that he who does not mind his belly will hardly mind anything else."
>
> Samuel Johnson

Food for Thought

*I*n all cases educate the conscience, enlist the will, supply good, wholesome food, and the change will be readily made, and the demand for flesh will soon cease. (*Ministry of Healing,* page 317)

> "There can be no more shameful carelessness than with the food we eat for life itself. When we exist without thought or thanksgiving we are not men, but beasts."
>
> M.F.K. Fisher

*A*nother pernicious habit is that of eating just before bedtime. The regular meals may have been taken; but because there is a sense of faintness, more food is eaten. By indulgence this wrong practice becomes a habit and often so firmly fixed that it is thought impossible to sleep without food. As a result of eating late suppers, the digestive process is continued through the sleeping hours. But though the stomach works constantly, its work is not properly accomplished. The sleep is often disturbed with unpleasant dreams, and in the morning the person awakes unrefreshed and with little relish for breakfast. When we lie down to rest, the stomach should have its work all done, that it, as well as the other organs of the body, may enjoy rest. For persons of sedentary habits, late suppers are particularly harmful. With them the disturbance created is often the beginning of disease that ends in death. (*Ministry of Healing,* page 303)

> "I consider the discovery of a dish which sustains our appetite and prolongs our pleasures as a far more interesting event than the discovery of a star."
>
> Henrion de Pensey

*S*ome wish that an exact rule could be prescribed for their diet. They overeat, and then regret it, and so they keep thinking about

Food for Thought

what they eat and drink. This is not as it should be. One person cannot lay down an exact rule for another. Everyone should exercise reason and self-control, and should act from principle. (*Ministry of Healing*, page 310)

> "The healthy stomach is nothing if it is not conservative. Few radicals have good digestions."
>
> Samuel Butler

When flesh food is discarded, its place should be supplied with a variety of grains, nuts, vegetables, and fruits that will be both nourishing and appetizing. This is especially necessary in the case of those who are weak or who are taxed with continuous labor. In some countries where poverty abounds, flesh is the cheapest food. Under these circumstances the change will be made with greater difficulty; but it can be effected. We should, however, consider the situation of the people and the power of lifelong habit, and should be careful not to urge even right ideas unduly. None should be urged to make the change abruptly. The place of meat should be supplied with wholesome foods that are inexpensive. In this matter very much depends on the cook. With care and skill, dishes may be prepared that will be both nutritious and appetizing, and will, to a great degree, take the place of flesh food. (*Ministry of Healing*, page 316)

> "The greatest delight the fields and woods minister is the suggestion of an occult relation between man and the vegetable. I am not alone and unacknowledged. They nod to me and I to them."
>
> Ralph Waldo Emerson

Food for Thought

EDUCATING CHILDREN

The home is the child's first school, and it is here that the foundation should be laid for a life of service. Its principles are to be taught not merely in theory. They are to shape the whole life training. (*Ministry of Healing*, page 400)

> "Play gives children a chance to practice what they are learning . . . They have to play with what they know to be true in order to find out more, and then they can use what they learn in new forms of play."
>
> — Fred Rogers

Let the youth advance as fast and as far as they can in the acquisition of knowledge. Let their field of study be as broad as their powers can compass. And, as they learn, let them impart their knowledge. It is thus that their minds will acquire discipline and power. It is the use they make of knowledge that determines the value of their education. To spend a long time in study, with no effort to impart what is gained, often proves a hindrance rather than a help to real development. In both the home and the school it should be the student's effort to learn how to study and how to impart the knowledge gained. Whatever his calling, he is to be both a learner and a teacher as long as life shall last. (*Ministry of Healing*, page 402)

> "One looks back with appreciation to the brilliant teachers, but with gratitude to those who touched our human feelings. The curriculum is so much necessary raw material, but warmth is the vital element for the growing plant and for the soul of the child."
>
> — Carl Jung

Food for Thought

Parents should early seek to interest their children in the study of physiology and should teach them its simpler principles. Teach them how best to preserve the physical, mental, and spiritual powers, and how to use their gifts so that their lives may bring blessing to one another and honor to God. This knowledge is invaluable to the young. An education in the things that concern life and health is more important to them than a knowledge of many of the sciences taught in the schools. (*Ministry of Healing*, page 385)

> "Let thy child's first lesson be obedience, and the second will be what thou wilt."
>
> Benjamin Franklin

Every child and every youth should have a knowledge of himself. He should understand the physical habitation that God has given him, and the laws by which it is kept in health. All should be thoroughly grounded in the common branches of education. And they should have industrial training that will make them men and women of practical ability, fitted for the duties of everyday life. To this should be added training and practical experience in various lines of missionary effort. (*Ministry of Healing*, page 402)

> "The object of education is to prepare the young to educate themselves throughout their lives."
>
> Robert Maynard Hutchins

EDUCATION FOR LIFE

True education includes the whole being. It teaches the right use of one's self. It enables us to make the best use of brain, bone, and muscle, of body, mind, and heart. The faculties of the mind, as the higher powers, are to rule the kingdom of the body. The natural appetites and passions are to be brought under the control of the conscience and the spiritual affections. (*Ministry of Healing*, page 398)

> "'Tis education forms the common mind: Just as a twig is bent, the tree's inclined."
>
> Alexander Pope

Many become inefficient by evading responsibilities for fear of failure. Thus they fail of gaining that education which results from experience, and which reading and study and all the advantages otherwise gained cannot give them. (*Ministry of Healing*, page 500)

> "Knowledge is not eating, and we cannot expect to devour and possess what we mean. Knowledge is recognition of something absent; it is a salutation, not an embrace."
>
> George Santayana

Let proper methods be taught to all who are willing to learn. If any do not wish you to speak to them of advanced ideas, let the lessons be given silently. Keep up the culture of your own land. Drop a word to your neighbors when you can, and let the harvest be eloquent in favor of right methods. Demonstrate what can be done with the land when properly worked. (*Ministry of Healing*, page 193)

Food for Thought

"Education is a progressive discovery of our ignorance."

Will Durant

What we need is knowledge that will strengthen mind and soul, that will make us better men and women. Heart education is of far more importance than mere book learning. It is well, even essential, to have a knowledge of the world in which we live; but if we leave eternity out of our reckoning, we shall make a failure from which we can never recover. (*Ministry of Healing,* page 450)

"The only purpose of education is to teach a student how to live his life—by developing his mind and equipping him to deal with reality. The training he needs is theoretical, i.e., conceptual. He has to be taught to think, to understand, to integrate, to prove. He has to be taught the essentials of the knowledge discovered in the past—and he has to be equipped to acquire further knowledge by his own effort."

Ayn Rand

Never think that you have learned enough, and that you may now relax your efforts. The cultivated mind is the measure of the man. Your education should continue during your lifetime; every day you should be learning and putting to practical use the knowledge gained. (*Ministry of Healing,* page 499)

"Knowledge is power."

Francis Bacon

The highest of all sciences is the science of soul saving. The greatest work to which human beings can aspire is the work of winning men from sin to holiness. For the accomplishment of this work, a broad foundation must be laid. A comprehensive education is needed—an education that will demand from parents and teachers such thought and effort as mere instruction in the sciences does not require. Something more is called for than the culture of the intellect. Education is not complete unless the body, the mind, and the heart are equally educated. The character must receive proper discipline for its fullest and highest development. All the faculties of mind and body are to be developed and rightly trained. It is a duty to cultivate and to exercise every power that will render us more efficient workers for God. (*Ministry of Healing*, page 398)

> "If you cannot read all your books, at any rate handle them, and, as it were, fondle them. Let them fall open as they will. Make a voyage of discovery, taking soundings of uncharted seas."
>
> Winston Churchill

EMOTIONS

It is not wise to look to ourselves and study our emotions. If we do this, the enemy will present difficulties and temptations that weaken faith and destroy courage. Closely to study our emotions and give way to our feelings is to entertain doubt and entangle ourselves in perplexity. (*Ministry of Healing*, page 249)

> "Never feel self-pity, the most destructive emotion there is. How awful to be caught up in the terrible squirrel cage of self."
>
> Millicent Fenwick

If impatient words are spoken to you, never reply in the same spirit. Remember that "a soft answer turneth away wrath." Proverbs 15:1. And there is wonderful power in silence. Words spoken in reply to one who is angry sometimes serve only to exasperate. But anger met with silence, in a tender, forbearing spirit, quickly dies away. (*Ministry of Healing,* page 486)

"Not to have control over the senses is like sailing in a rudderless ship, bound to break to pieces on coming in contact with the very first rock."

Mahatma Gandhi

We should not allow our feelings to be easily wounded. We are to live, not to guard our feelings or our reputation, but to save souls. As we become interested in the salvation of souls we cease to mind the little differences that so often arise in our association with one another. (*Ministry of Healing,* page 485)

"The most repressed and denied aspects of our soul . . . [are] often the treasure that lies buried in the darkness."

Carl Jung

EXERCISE FOR THE BODY

Inactivity is a fruitful cause of disease. Exercise quickens and equalizes the circulation of the blood, but in idleness the blood does not circulate freely, and the changes in it, so necessary to life and health, do not take place. The skin, too, becomes inactive. Impurities are not expelled as they would be if the circulation had been quickened by vigorous exercise, the skin kept in a healthy condition, and the lungs fed with plenty of pure, fresh air. This state of the system throws a double burden on the excretory organs, and disease is the result. (*Ministry of Healing,* page 238)

Food for Thought

> "You can develop good judgment as you do the muscles of your body—by judicious, daily exercise."
>
> — Grenville Kleiser

*M*inisters, teachers, students, and other brain workers often suffer from illness as the result of severe mental taxation, unrelieved by physical exercise. What these persons need is a more active life. Strictly temperate habits, combined with proper exercise, would ensure both mental and physical vigor, and would give power of endurance to all brain workers. (*Ministry of Healing*, page 238)

> "The higher your energy level, the more efficient your body. The more efficient your body, the better you feel and the more you will use your talent to produce outstanding results."
>
> — Anthony Robbins

*A*ction is a law of our being. Every organ of the body has its appointed work, upon the performance of which its development and strength depend. The normal action of all the organs gives strength and vigor, while the tendency of disuse is toward decay and death. Bind up an arm, even for a few weeks, then free it from its bands, and you will see that it is weaker than the one you have been using moderately during the same time. Inactivity produces the same effect upon the whole muscular system. (*Ministry of Healing*, page 237)

> "Trouble springs from idleness, and grievous toil from needless ease."
>
> — Benjamin Franklin

*I*n all these cases well-directed physical exercise would prove an effective remedial agent. In some cases it is indispensable to the

Food for Thought

recovery of health. The will goes with the labor of the hands; and what these invalids need is to have the will aroused. When the will is dormant, the imagination becomes abnormal, and it is impossible to resist disease. (*Ministry of Healing*, page 239)

> "The preservation of health is a duty. Few seem conscious that there is such a thing as physical morality."
>
> — Herbert Spencer

Those whose habits are sedentary should, when the weather will permit, exercise in the open air every day, summer or winter. Walking is preferable to riding or driving, for it brings more of the muscles into exercise. The lungs are forced into healthy action, since it is impossible to walk briskly without inflating them. (*Ministry of Healing*, page 240)

> "Lack of activity destroys the good condition of every human being, while movement and methodical physical exercise save it and preserve it."
>
> — Plato

FAITH IN GOD

Faith is a mightier conqueror than death. If the sick can be led to fix their eyes in faith upon the Mighty Healer, we shall see wonderful results. It will bring life to the body and to the soul. (*Ministry of Healing*, page 62)

Food for Thought

> "Sweet souls around us watch us still, press nearer to our side; into our thoughts, into our prayers, with gentle helpings glide."
>
> — Harriet Beecher Stowe

Some are continually anxious lest their food, however simple and healthful, may hurt them. To these let me say, Do not think that your food will injure you; do not think about it at all. Eat according to your best judgment; and when you have asked the Lord to bless the food for the strengthening of your body, believe that He hears your prayer, and be at rest. (*Ministry of Healing*, page 321)

> "We need to find God, and he cannot be found in noise and restlessness. God is the friend of silence. See how nature, trees, flowers, grass grows in silence; see the stars, the moon and the sun, how they move in silence . . . we need silence to be able to touch souls."
>
> — Mother Teresa

The knowledge that man is to be a temple for God, a habitation for the revealing of His glory, should be the highest incentive to the care and development of our physical powers. Fearfully and wonderfully has the Creator wrought in the human frame, and He bids us make it our study, understand its needs, and act our part in preserving it from harm and defilement. (*Ministry of Healing*, page 271)

> "For when the one Great Scorer comes to mark against your name, he writes—not whether you won or lost—but how you played the Game."
>
> — Grantland Rice

Food for Thought

The body is to be brought into subjection. The higher powers of the being are to rule. The passions are to be controlled by the will, which is itself to be under the control of God. The kingly power of reason, sanctified by divine grace, is to bear sway in our lives. (*Ministry of Healing*, page 130)

> "One Universe made up of all that is; and one God in it all, and one principle of Being, and one Law, the Reason, shared by all thinking creatures, and one Truth."
>
> Marcus Aurelius

God desires to bring men into direct relation with Himself. In all His dealings with human beings He recognizes the principle of personal responsibility. He seeks to encourage a sense of personal dependence and to impress the need of personal guidance. He desires to bring the human into association with the divine, that men may be transformed into the divine likeness. Satan works to thwart this purpose. He seeks to encourage dependence upon men. When minds are turned away from God, the tempter can bring them under his rule. He can control humanity. (*Ministry of Healing*, page 242)

> "Each of us has a responsibility for being alive: one responsibility to creation, of which we are a part, another to the creator a debt we repay by trying to extend our areas of comprehension."
>
> Maya Angelou

Great wisdom is needed in dealing with diseases caused through the mind. A sore, sick heart, a discouraged mind, needs mild treatment. Many times some living home trouble is, like a canker, eating to the very soul and weakening the life force. And sometimes it is the case that remorse for sin undermines the

Food for Thought

constitution and unbalances the mind. It is through tender sympathy that this class of invalids can be benefited. The physician should first gain their confidence and then point them to the Great Healer. If their faith can be directed to the True Physician, and they can have confidence that He has undertaken their case, this will bring relief to the mind and often give health to the body. (*Ministry of Healing*, page 244)

> "The creator of this universe made man in the beginning out of the ground. The different properties which are found in the earth are found in man, and the fruits, grains, nuts, and vegetables contain the same elements which are in the earth, and in man. When these fruits, grains, nuts, and vegetables are eaten in their natural state and not perverted and robbed of their life-giving properties in their preparation, health, beauty, and happiness will be the sure reward. The scripture which says, 'My people are destroyed for lack of knowledge,' is surely being fulfilled."
>
> Jethro Kloss

For every trial, God has provided help. When Israel in the desert came to the bitter waters of Marah, Moses cried unto the Lord. The Lord did not provide some new remedy; He called attention to that which was at hand. A shrub which He had created was to be cast into the fountain to make the water pure and sweet. When this was done, the people drank of the water and were refreshed. In every trial, if we seek Him, Christ will give us help. Our eyes will be opened to discern the healing promises recorded in His word. The Holy Spirit will teach us how to appropriate every blessing that will be an antidote to grief. For every bitter draft that is placed to our lips, we shall find a branch of healing. (*Ministry of Healing*, page 248)

> "God's gifts put man's best dreams to shame."
>
> Elizabeth Barrett Browning

Food for Thought

FAITH IN SELF

*I*t is not God's purpose that any human being should yield his mind and will to the control of another, becoming a passive instrument in his hands. No one is to merge his individuality in that of another. (*Ministry of Healing,* page 242)

> "Do not go where the path may lead, go instead where there is no path and leave a trail."
>
> Ralph Waldo Emerson

*I*t is our own character and experience that determine our influence upon others. (*Ministry of Healing,* page 469)

> "I prefer to be true to myself, even at the hazard of incurring the ridicule of others, rather than to be false, and to incur my own abhorrence."
>
> Frederick Douglass

*M*any who are qualified to do excellent work accomplish little because they attempt little. Thousands pass through life as if they had no great object for which to live, no high standard to reach. One reason for this is the low estimate which they place upon themselves. (*Ministry of Healing,* page 498)

> "The consuming desire of most human beings is deliberately to plant their whole life in the hands of some other person. I would describe this method of searching for happiness as immature. Development of character consists solely in moving toward self-sufficiency."
>
> Quentin Crisp

We cannot afford to let our spirits chafe over any real or supposed wrong done to ourselves. Self is the enemy we most need to fear. No form of vice has a more baleful effect upon the character than has human passion not under the control of the Holy Spirit. No other victory we can gain will be so precious as the victory gained over self. (*Ministry of Healing*, page 485)

"I want you to be everything that's you, deep at the center of your being."

Confucius

FAMILY

Children as well as parents have important duties in the home. They should be taught that they are a part of the home firm. They are fed and clothed and loved and cared for, and they should respond to these many mercies by bearing their share of the home burdens and bringing all the happiness possible into the family of which they are members. (*Ministry of Healing*, page 394)

"The family is one of nature's masterpieces."

George Santayana

The family tie is the closest, the most tender and sacred, of any on earth. It was designed to be a blessing to mankind. And it is a blessing wherever the marriage covenant is entered into intelligently, in the fear of God, and with due consideration for its responsibilities. (*Ministry of Healing*, page 356)

Food for Thought

"The first half of our lives is ruined by our parents and the second half by our children."

Clarence Darrow

Very early the lesson of helpfulness should be taught the child. As soon as strength and reasoning power are sufficiently developed, he should be given duties to perform in the home. He should be encouraged in trying to help father and mother, encouraged to deny and to control himself, to put other's happiness and convenience before his own, to watch for opportunities to cheer and assist brothers and sisters and playmates, and to show kindness to the aged, the sick, and the unfortunate. The more fully the spirit of true ministry pervades the home, the more fully it will be developed in the lives of the children. They will learn to find joy in service and sacrifice for the good of others. (*Ministry of Healing*, page 401)

"Love the family! Defend and promote it as the basic cell of human society; nurture it as the prime sanctuary of life. Give great care to the preparation of engaged couples and be close to young married couples, so that they will be for their children and the whole community an eloquent testimony of God's love."

Pope John Paul II

If you are blessed with God-fearing parents, seek counsel of them. Open to them your hopes and plans, learn the lessons which their life experiences have taught, and you will be saved many a heartache. Above all, make Christ your counselor. Study His word with prayer. (*Ministry of Healing*, page 359)

"The most important thing a father can do for his children is to love their mother."

Henry Ward Beecher

Food for Thought

The husband and father is the head of the household. The wife looks to him for love and sympathy, and for aid in the training of the children; and this is right. The children are his as well as hers, and he is equally interested in their welfare. The children look to their father for support and guidance; he needs to have a right conception of life and of the influences and associations that should surround his family; above all, he should be controlled by the love and fear of God and by the teaching of His word, that he may guide the feet of his children in the right way. (*Ministry of Healing*, page 390)

> "In a home that's a refuge, chores can wait a few moments while a child strokes and confides in a cat. A father can watch television with a bowl of popcorn in his lap and choose not to answer the phone. A mother can relax in a tub undisturbed while her worries melt away."
>
> Mimi Wilson and Mary Beth Lagerborg

The husband and father who is morose, selfish, and overbearing, is not only unhappy himself, but he casts gloom upon all the inmates of his home. He will reap the result in seeing his wife dispirited and sickly, and his children marred with his own unlovely temper. (*Ministry of Healing*, page 374)

> "The family—that dear octopus from whose tentacles we never quite escape, nor, in our inmost hearts, ever quite wish to."
>
> Dodie Smith

Children are sometimes tempted to chafe under restraint; but in afterlife they will bless their parents for the faithful care and strict watchfulness that guarded and guided them in their years of inexperience. (*Ministry of Healing*, page 394)

Food for Thought

"The family is the corner stone of our society. More than any other force it shapes the attitude, the hopes, the ambitions, and the values of the child. And when the family collapses it is the children that are usually damaged. When it happens on a massive scale the community itself is crippled. So, unless we work to strengthen the family, to create conditions under which most parents will stay together, all the rest—schools, playgrounds, and public assistance, and private concern—will never be enough."

Lyndon Baines Johnson

Brought up under the wise and loving guidance of a true home, children will have no desire to wander away in search of pleasure and companionship. Evil will not attract them. The spirit that prevails in the home will mold their characters; they will form habits and principles that will be a strong defense against temptation when they shall leave the home shelter and take their place in the world. (*Ministry of Healing*, page 394)

"Individual commitment to a group effort—that is what makes a team work, a company work, a society work, a civilization work."

Vince Lombardi

The restoration and uplifting of humanity begins in the home. The work of parents underlies every other. Society is composed of families, and is what the heads of families make it. Out of the heart are "the issues of life" (Proverbs 4:23); and the heart of the community, of the church, and of the nation is the household. The well-being of society, the success of the church, the prosperity of the nation, depend upon home influences. (*Ministry of Healing*, page 349)

"Call it a clan, call it a network, call it a tribe, call it a family. Whatever you call it, whoever you are, you need one."

Jane Howard

FOOD DANGERS

In many places fish become so contaminated by the filth on which they feed as to be a cause of disease. This is especially the case where the fish come in contact with the sewage of large cities. The fish that are fed on the contents of the drains may pass into distant waters and may be caught where the water is pure and fresh. Thus when used as food they bring disease and death on those who do not suspect the danger. (*Ministry of Healing*, page 314)

"Nearly 70 percent of children who consume a typical American diet have fatty deposits in their coronary arteries—the earliest sign of coronary heart disease—by the age of twelve."

Dr. Charles Attwood

Often intemperance begins in the home. By the use of rich, unhealthful food the digestive organs are weakened, and a desire is created for food that is still more stimulating. Thus the appetite is educated to crave continually something stronger. The demand for stimulants becomes more frequent and more difficult to resist. The system becomes more or less filled with poison, and the more debilitated it becomes, the greater is the desire for these things. One step in the wrong direction prepares the way for another. Many who would not be guilty of placing on their table wine or liquor of any kind will load their table with food which creates such a thirst for strong drink that to resist the temptation is almost impossible. Wrong habits of eating and drinking destroy the health and prepare the way for drunkenness. (*Ministry of Healing,* page 334)

> "Every sip of cow's milk contains virus, pus, bacteria, powerful growth hormones, proteins that cause allergies, antibiotics, pesticides, fat, cholesterol, and dioxins. For thousands of lines of converging evidence proving that milk does not do the body any good, visit notmilk.com on the Internet."
>
> Robert "Notmilkman" Cohen

These unpleasant symptoms are felt because nature has accomplished her work at an unnecessary outlay of vital force and is thoroughly exhausted. The stomach is saying, "Give me rest." But with many the faintness is interpreted as a demand for more food; so instead of giving the stomach rest, another burden is placed upon it. As a consequence the digestive organs are often worn out when they should be capable of doing good work. (*Ministry of Healing,* page 307)

> "Never eat more than you can lift."
>
> Miss Piggy

Far too much sugar is ordinarily used in food. Cakes, sweet puddings, pastries, jellies, jams, are active causes of indigestion. Especially harmful are the custards and puddings in which milk, eggs, and sugar are the chief ingredients. The free use of milk and sugar taken together should be avoided. (*Ministry of Healing,* page 301)

Food for Thought

"He that eats till he is sick must fast till he is well."

English proverb

FOOD FOR HEALTH

Nuts and nut foods are coming largely into use to take the place of flesh meats. With nuts may be combined grains, fruits, and some roots, to make foods that are healthful and nourishing. Care should be taken, however, not to use too large a proportion of nuts. Those who realize ill effects from the use of nut foods may find the difficulty removed by attending to this precaution. It should be remembered, too, that some nuts are not so wholesome as others. Almonds are preferable to peanuts, but peanuts in limited quantities, used in connection with grains, are nourishing and digestible. (*Ministry of Healing*, page 298)

> "It seems a pity that cheap humor and poor jokes should be laid do heavily on such an excellent serviceable fruit as the prune—which is always good, always in season, and capable of use in so many ways."
>
> Artemus Ward

Wherever dried fruits, such as raisins, prunes, apples, pears, peaches, and apricots are obtainable at moderate prices, it will be found that they can be used as staple articles of diet much more freely than is customary, with the best results to the health and vigor of all classes of workers. (*Ministry of Healing*, page 299)

Food for Thought

"Nothing will benefit human health and increase chances for survival of life on Earth as much as the evolution to a vegetarian diet."

Albert Einstein

Grains, fruits, nuts, and vegetables constitute the diet chosen for us by our Creator. These foods, prepared in as simple and natural a manner as possible, are the most healthful and nourishing. They impart a strength, a power of endurance, and a vigor of intellect that are not afforded by a more complex and stimulating diet. (*Ministry of Healing,* page 296)

"Scientific data suggest positive relationships between a vegetarian diet and reduced risk for several chronic degenerative diseases and conditions, including obesity, coronary artery disease, hypertension, diabetes mellitus, and some types of cancer."

Journal of the American Dietetic Association

If we plan wisely, that which is most conducive to health can be secured in almost every land. The various preparations of rice, wheat, corn, and oats are sent abroad everywhere, also beans, peas, and lentils. These, with native or imported fruits, and the variety of vegetables that grow in each locality, give an opportunity to select a diet that is complete without the use of flesh meats. (*Ministry of Healing,* page 299)

"Did you ever stop to taste a carrot? Not just eat it, but taste it? You can't taste the beauty and energy of the earth in a Twinkie."

Astrid Alauda

Food for Thought

GOD'S GIFTS AND LOVE

God loves the beautiful. He has clothed the earth and the heavens with beauty, and with a Father's joy. He watches the delight of His children in the things that He has made. He desires us to surround our homes with the beauty of natural things. (*Ministry of Healing*, page 370)

> "And God said, 'Behold, I have given you every herb bearing seed, which is upon the face of all the earth, and every tree, in the which is the fruit of a tree yielding seed; to you it shall be for meat.'"
>
> Genesis 1:29

It is a law of nature that our thoughts and feelings are encouraged and strengthened as we give them utterance. While words express thoughts, it is also true that thoughts follow words. If we would give more expression to our faith, rejoice more in the blessings that we know we have, the great mercy and love of God, we should have more faith and greater joy. No tongue can express, no finite mind can conceive, the blessing that results from appreciating the goodness and love of God. Even on earth we may have joy as a wellspring, never failing, because fed by the streams that flow from the throne of God. (*Ministry of Healing*, page 251)

> "When one has tasted it (watermelon) he knows what the angels eat."
>
> Mark Twain

The requirements of God must be brought home to the conscience. Men and women must be awakened to the duty of self-mastery, the need of purity, freedom from every depraving

Food for Thought

appetite and defiling habit. They need to be impressed with the fact that all their powers of mind and body are the gift of God, and are to be preserved in the best possible condition for His service. (*Ministry of Healing,* page 130)

> "A baby is God's opinion that the world should go on."
>
> Carl Sandburg

In nature may always be found something to divert the attention of the sick from themselves and direct their thoughts to God. Surrounded by His wonderful works, their minds are uplifted from the things that are seen to the things that are unseen. The beauty of nature leads them to think of the heavenly home, where there will be nothing to mar the loveliness, nothing to taint or destroy, nothing to cause disease or death. (*Ministry of Healing,* page 265)

> "Gentlemen . . . look around you at the gifts of God, the clear sky, the pure air, the tender grass, the birds; nature is beautiful and sinless, and we, only we, are godless and foolish, and we don't understand that life is a paradise, for we have only to understand that and it will at once be fulfilled in all its beauty, we shall embrace each other and weep."
>
> Fyodor Dostoevsky

Let physicians and nurses draw from the things of nature, lessons teaching of God. Let them point the patients to Him whose hand has made the lofty trees, the grass, and the flowers, encouraging them to see in every bud and flower an expression of His love for His children. He who cares for the birds and the flowers will care for the beings formed in His own image. (*Ministry of Healing,* page 266)

Food for Thought

"Never lose an opportunity of seeing anything that is beautiful; for beauty is God's handwriting—a wayside sacrament. Welcome it in every fair face, in every fair sky, in every fair flower, and thank God for it as a cup of blessing."

Ralph Waldo Emerson

HAPPINESS

Courage, hope, faith, sympathy, love, promote health and prolong life. A contented mind, a cheerful spirit, is health to the body and strength to the soul. (*Ministry of Healing*, page 241)

"Life is made up of small pleasures. Happiness is made up of those tiny successes. The big ones come too infrequently. And if you don't collect all these tiny successes, the big ones don't really mean anything."

Norman Lear

Good deeds are twice a blessing, benefiting both the giver and the receiver of the kindness. The consciousness of right-doing is one of the best medicines for diseased bodies and minds. When the mind is free and happy from a sense of duty well done and the satisfaction of giving happiness to others, the cheering, uplifting influence brings new life to the whole being. (*Ministry of Healing*, page 257)

Food for Thought

"A sound mind in a sound body, is a short, but full description of a happy state in this World: he that has these two, has little more to wish for; and he that wants either of them, will be little the better for anything else."

John Locke

Nothing tends more to promote health of body and of soul than does a spirit of gratitude and praise. It is a positive duty to resist melancholy, discontented thoughts and feelings—as much a duty as it is to pray. If we are heaven-bound, how can we go as a band of mourners, groaning and complaining all along the way to our Father's house? (*Ministry of Healing*, page 251)

"To live content with small means; to seek elegance rather than luxury, and refinement rather than fashion; to be worthy, not respectable, and wealthy, not rich; to listen to stars and birds, babes and sages, with open heart; to study hard; to think quietly, act frankly, talk gently, await occasions, hurry never; in a word, to let the spiritual, unbidden and unconscious, grow up through the common—this is my symphony."

William Henry Channing

But remember that happiness will not be found in shutting yourselves up to yourselves, satisfied to pour out all your affection upon each other. Seize upon every opportunity for contributing to the happiness of those around you. Remember that true joy can be found only in unselfish service. (*Ministry of Healing*, page 362)

Food for Thought

> "Happiness is the only sanction of life; where happiness fails, existence remains a mad and lamentable experiment."
>
> George Santayana

HAPPY MARRIAGES

The choice of a life companion should be such as best to secure physical, mental, and spiritual well-being for parents and for their children—such as will enable both parents and children to bless their fellow men and to honor their Creator. (*Ministry of Healing*, page 357)

> "Let me strive to be as true to her as she is to me. Let me too be loving, kind, and thoughtful. Especially let me not permit the passion I have to see constant improvement in those I love, to be so blind in its eagerness as to wound a nature so tenderly sensitive as I know I sometimes have done. This is indeed life. The love of wedded wife! Can anything enjoyed on earth be a source of truer, purer happiness—happiness more unalloyed than this? Blessings on his head who first invented marriage!"
>
> Rutherford Birchard Hayes

Around every family there is a sacred circle that should be kept unbroken. Within this circle no other person has a right to come. Let not the husband or the wife permit another to share the confidences that belong solely to themselves. (*Ministry of Healing*, page 361)

Food for Thought

"A man without a wife is like a vase without flowers."

African proverb

However carefully and wisely marriage may have been entered into, few couples are completely united when the marriage ceremony is performed. The real union of the two in wedlock is the work of the after years. (*Ministry of Healing*, page 359)

"Love before marriage is absolutely necessary."

Samuel Richardson

Under such guidance let a young woman accept as a life companion only one who possesses pure, manly traits of character, one who is diligent, aspiring, and honest, one who loves and fears God. Let a young man seek one to stand by his side who is fitted to bear her share of life's burdens, one whose influence will ennoble and refine him, and who will make him happy in her love. (*Ministry of Healing*, page 359)

"That quiet mutual gaze of a trusting husband and wife is like the first moment of rest or refuge from a great weariness or a great danger."

George Eliot (Mary Anne Evans)

HEALING NATURALLY

Pure air, sunlight, abstemiousness, rest, exercise, proper diet, the use of water, trust in divine power—these are the true remedies. Every person should have a knowledge of nature's

Food for Thought

remedial agencies and how to apply them. It is essential both to understand the principles involved in the treatment of the sick and to have a practical training that will enable one rightly to use this knowledge. (*Ministry of Healing,* page 127)

> "Flowers always make people better, happier, and more helpful: they are sunshine, food and medicine to the soul."
>
> Luther Burbank

Most persons would receive benefit from a cool or tepid bath every day, morning or evening. Instead of increasing the liability to take cold, a bath, properly taken, fortifies against cold, because it improves the circulation; the blood is brought to the surface, and a more easy and regular flow is obtained. The mind and the body are alike invigorated. The muscles become more flexible, the intellect is made brighter. The bath is a soother of the nerves. Bathing helps the bowels, the stomach, and the liver, giving health and energy to each, and it promotes digestion. (*Ministry of Healing,* page 276)

> Better to hunt in fields, for health unsought
> Than fee the doctor for a nauseous draught.
> The wise for cure on exercise depend;
> God never made his work for man to mend.
>
> John Dryden

The more the patient can be kept out of doors, the less care will he require. The more cheerful his surroundings, the more helpful will he be. Shut up in the house, be it ever so elegantly furnished, he will grow fretful and gloomy. Surround him with the beautiful things of nature; place him where he can see the flowers growing and hear the birds singing, and his heart will break into song in harmony with the songs of the birds. Relief will come to body and mind. The intellect will be awakened, the imagination quickened, and the mind prepared to appreciate the beauty of God's word. (*Ministry of Healing*, page 265)

> "The gods created certain kinds of beings to replenish our bodies . . . they are the trees and the plants and the seeds."
>
> Plato

To the chronic invalid, nothing so tends to restore health and happiness as living amid attractive country surroundings. Here the most helpless ones can sit or lie in the sunshine or in the shade of the trees. They have only to lift their eyes to see above them the beautiful foliage. A sweet sense of restfulness and refreshing comes over them as they listen to the murmuring of the breezes. The drooping spirits revive. The waning strength is recruited. Unconsciously the mind becomes peaceful, the fevered pulse more calm and regular. As the sick grow stronger, they will venture to take a few steps to gather some of the lovely flowers, precious messengers of God's love to His afflicted family here below. (*Ministry of Healing*, page 264)

> "Let your food be your medicine, and your medicine be your food."
>
> Hippocrates

The use of natural remedies requires an amount of care and effort that many are not willing to give. Nature's process of healing and upbuilding is gradual, and to the impatient it seems slow. The surrender of hurtful indulgences requires sacrifice. But in the end it will be found that nature, untrammeled, does her work wisely and well. Those who persevere in obedience to her laws will reap the reward in health of body and health of mind. (*Ministry of Healing*, page 127)

Food for Thought

"Water has no taste, no color, no odor; it cannot be defined, art relished while ever mysterious. Not necessary to life, but rather life itself. It fills us with a gratification that exceeds the delight of the senses."

Antoine de Saint Exupéry

Physicians and nurses should encourage their patients to be much in the open air. Outdoor life is the only remedy that many invalids need. It has a wonderful power to heal diseases caused by the excitements and excesses of fashionable life, a life that weakens and destroys the powers of body, mind, and soul. (*Ministry of Healing,* page 264)

"Let nothing which can be treated by diet be treated by other means."

Moses Maimonides

In health and in sickness, pure water is one of heaven's choicest blessings. Its proper use promotes health. It is the beverage which God provided to quench the thirst of animals and man. Drunk freely, it helps to supply the necessities of the system and assists nature to resist disease. The external application of water is one of the easiest and most satisfactory ways of regulating the circulation of the blood. A cold or cool bath is an excellent tonic. Warm baths open the pores and thus aid in the elimination of impurities. Both warm and neutral baths soothe the nerves and equalize the circulation. (*Ministry of Healing,* page 237)

Food for Thought

"To have a renewed body, you must be willing to have new perceptions that give rise to new solutions. Instead of consciously creating disease, we could be consciously creating health. When the mind is peaceful, inner energies wake up and work miracles for us—without any conscious effort on your part."

Deepak Chopra

One of the surest hindrances to the recovery of the sick is the centering of attention upon themselves. Many invalids feel that everyone should give them sympathy and help, when what they need is to have their attention turned away from themselves, to think of and care for others. (*Ministry of Healing,* page 256)

"Sunshine is delicious . . . wind braces us up."

John Ruskin

Such exercise would in many cases be better for the health than medicine. Physicians often advise their patients to take an ocean voyage, to go to some mineral spring, or to visit different places for change of climate, when in most cases if they would eat temperately, and take cheerful, healthful exercise, they would recover health and would save time and money. (*Ministry of Healing,* page 240)

"One must not forget that recovery is brought about not by the physician, but by the sick man himself. He heals himself, by his own power, exactly as he walks by means of his own power, or eats, or thinks, breathes or sleeps."

Georg Groddeck

But many have never learned by experience the beneficial effects of the proper use of water, and they are afraid of it. Water treatments are not appreciated as they should be, and to apply

Food for Thought

them skillfully requires work that many are unwilling to perform. But none should feel excused for ignorance or indifference on this subject. There are many ways in which water can be applied to relieve pain and check disease. All should become intelligent in its use in simple home treatments. Mothers, especially, should know how to care for their families in both health and sickness. (*Ministry of Healing*, page 237)

> "Let the clean air blow the cobwebs from your body. Air is medicine."
>
> Lillian Russell

Some make themselves sick by overwork. For these, rest, freedom from care, and a spare diet, are essential to restoration of health. To those who are brain weary and nervous because of continual labor and close confinement, a visit to the country, where they can live a simple, carefree life, coming in close contact with the things of nature, will be most helpful. Roaming through the fields and the woods, picking the flowers, listening to the songs of the birds, will do far more than any other agency toward their recovery. (*Ministry of Healing*, page 236)

> "I don't think of all the misery, but of the beauty that still remains. My advice is: Go outside to the fields, enjoy nature and the sunshine, go out and try to recapture happiness in yourself and in God. Think of all the beauty that's still left in and around you and be happy."
>
> Anne Frank

Food for Thought

HOME ENVIRONMENT

In the building of houses it is especially important to secure thorough ventilation and plenty of sunlight. Let there be a current of air and an abundance of light in every room in the house. Sleeping rooms should be so arranged as to have a free circulation of air day and night. No room is fit to be occupied as a sleeping room unless it can be thrown open daily to the air and sunshine. In most countries bedrooms need to be supplied with conveniences for heating, that they may be thoroughly warmed and dried in cold or wet weather. (*Ministry of Healing*, page 274)

> Mid pleasures and palaces though we may roam,
> Be it ever so humble, there's no place like home!
> A charm from the skies seems to hallow us there,
> Which sought through the world is ne'er met with elsewhere.
>
> J. Howard Payne

Perfect cleanliness, plenty of sunlight, careful attention to sanitation in every detail of the home life, are essential to freedom from disease and to the cheerfulness and vigor of the inmates of the home. (*Ministry of Healing*, page 276)

> "The strength of a nation derives from the integrity of the home."
>
> Confucius

Let the homemakers resolve to live on a wiser plan. Let it be your first aim to make a pleasant home. Be sure to provide the facilities that will lighten labor and promote health and comfort. (*Ministry of Healing*, page 369)

Food for Thought

"The house of every one is to him as his castle and fortress, as well for his defense against injury and violence as for his repose."

Sir Edward Coke

The home training should be supplemented by the work of the school. The development of the whole being, physical, mental, and spiritual, and the teaching of service and sacrifice, should be kept constantly in view. (*Ministry of Healing,* page 401)

"What is most important and valuable about the home as a base for children's growth into the world is not that it is a better school than the schools, but that it isn't a school at all."

John Holt

In building, many make careful provision for their plants and flowers. The greenhouse or window devoted to their use is warm and sunny; for without warmth, air, and sunshine, plants would not live and flourish. If these conditions are necessary to the life of plants, how much more necessary are they for our own health and that of our families and guests! (*Ministry of Healing,* page 275)

"Home is where one starts from."

T.S. Eliot

Furnish your home with things plain and simple, things that will bear handling, that can be easily kept clean, and that can be replaced without great expense. By exercising taste, you can make a very simple home attractive and inviting, if love and contentment are there. (*Ministry of Healing,* page 370)

Food for Thought

"Where we love is home—home that our feet may leave, but not our hearts."

Oliver Wendell Holmes, Sr.

If we would have our homes the abiding place of health and happiness we must place them above the miasma and fog of the lowlands, and give free entrance to heaven's life-giving agencies. Dispense with heavy curtains, open the windows and the blinds, allow no vines, however beautiful, to shade the windows, and permit no trees to stand so near the house as to shut out the sunshine. The sunlight may fade the drapery and the carpets, and tarnish the picture frames; but it will bring a healthy glow to the cheeks of the children. (*Ministry of Healing*, page 275)

"You can never go home again, but the truth is you can never leave home, so it's all right."

Maya Angelou

LIVING SUPERFICIALLY

Our artificial habits deprive us of many blessings and much enjoyment, and unfit us for living the most useful lives. Elaborate and expensive furnishings are a waste not only of money, but of that which is a thousandfold more precious. They bring into the home a heavy burden of care and labor and perplexity. (*Ministry of Healing*, page 367)

Food for Thought

"Economy, prudence, and a simple life are the sure masters of need, and will often accomplish that which, their opposites, with a fortune at hand, will fail to do so."

Clara Barton

Life in the cities is false and artificial. The intense passion for money getting, the whirl of excitement and pleasure seeking, the thirst for display, the luxury and extravagance, all are forces that, with the great masses of mankind, are turning the mind from life's true purpose. They are opening the door to a thousand evils. Upon the youth they have almost irresistible power. (*Ministry of Healing*, page 364)

"Power is the faculty or capacity to act, the strength and potency to accomplish something. It is the vital energy to make choices and decisions. It also includes the capacity to overcome deeply embedded habits and to cultivate higher, more effective ones."

Stephen R. Covey

Those who have but a partial understanding of the principles of reform are often the most rigid, not only in carrying out their views themselves, but in urging them on their families and their neighbors. The effect of their mistaken reforms, as seen in their own ill-health, and their efforts to force their views upon others, give many a false idea of dietetic reform, and lead them to reject it altogether. (*Ministry of Healing*, page 318)

"Joy has nothing to do with material things, or with man's outward circumstance . . . A man living in the lap of luxury can be wretched, and a man in the depths of poverty can overflow with joy."

William Barclay

Food for Thought

What are the conditions in many homes, even where resources are limited and the work of the household rests chiefly on the mother? The best rooms are furnished in a style beyond the means of the occupants and unsuited to their convenience and enjoyment. There are expensive carpets, elaborately carved and daintily upholstered furniture, and delicate drapery. Tables, mantels, and every other available space are crowded with ornaments, and the walls are covered with pictures, until the sight becomes wearying. And what an amount of work is required to keep all these in order and free from dust! This work, and the other artificial habits of the family in its conformity to fashion, demand of the housewife unending toil. (*Ministry of Healing,* page 367)

> "No diet will remove all the fat from your body because the brain is entirely fat. Without a brain, you might look good, but all you could do is run for public office."
>
> George Bernard Shaw

Simplicity, self-denial, economy, lessons so essential for the poor to learn, often seem to them difficult and unwelcome. The example and spirit of the world is constantly exciting and fostering pride, love of display, self-indulgence, prodigality, and idleness. These evils bring thousands to penury and prevent thousands more from rising out of degradation and wretchedness. (*Ministry of Healing,* page 196)

> "Many persons have a wrong idea of what constitutes true happiness. It is not attained through self-gratification but through fidelity to a worthy purpose."
>
> Helen Keller

If he does not observe the laws that govern his own being, if he chooses selfish gratification above soundness of mind and body, does he not thereby declare himself unfit to be entrusted with the responsibility of human lives? (*Ministry of Healing*, page 134)

> "That man is richest whose pleasures are cheapest."
>
> Henry David Thoreau

LOVE

The most careful cultivation of the outward proprieties of life is not sufficient to shut out all fretfulness, harsh judgment, and unbecoming speech. True refinement will never be revealed so long as self is considered as the supreme object. Love must dwell in the heart. Love imparts to its possessor grace, propriety, and comeliness of deportment. It illuminates the countenance and subdues the voice; it refines and elevates the whole being. (*Ministry of Healing*, page 490)

> "Love seems the swiftest, but it is the slowest of all growths. No man or woman really knows what perfect love is until they have been married a quarter of a century."
>
> Mark Twain

*L*et each give love rather than exact it. Cultivate that which is noblest in yourselves, and be quick to recognize the good qualities in each other. The consciousness of being appreciated is a wonderful stimulus and satisfaction. Sympathy and respect

Food for Thought

encourage the striving after excellence, and love itself increases as it stimulates to nobler aims. (*Ministry of Healing,* page 361)

"When we are motivated by goals that have deep meaning, by dreams that need completion, by pure love that needs expressing, then we truly live life."

Greg Anderson

As life with its burden of perplexity and care meets the newly wedded pair, the romance with which imagination so often invests marriage disappears. Husband and wife learn each other's character as it was impossible to learn it in their previous association. This is a most critical period in their experience. The happiness and usefulness of their whole future life depend upon their taking a right course now. Often they discern in each other unsuspected weaknesses and defects; but the hearts that love has united will discern excellencies also heretofore unknown. Let all seek to discover the excellencies rather than the defects. Often it is our own attitude, the atmosphere that surrounds ourselves, which determines what will be revealed to us in another. There are many who regard the expression of love as a weakness, and they maintain a reserve that repels others. This spirit checks the current of sympathy. As the social and generous impulses are repressed, they wither, and the heart becomes desolate and cold. We should beware of this error. Love cannot long exist without expression. Let not the heart of one connected with you starve for the want of kindness and sympathy. (*Ministry of Healing,* page 360)

"A blessed thing it is for any man or woman to have a friend, one human soul whom we can trust utterly, who knows the best and worst of us, and who loves us in spite of all our faults."

Charles Kingsley

Food for Thought

MARITAL ADVICE

Let the husband aid his wife by his sympathy and unfailing affection. If he wishes to keep her fresh and gladsome, so that she will be as sunshine in the home, let him help her bear her burdens. His kindness and loving courtesy will be to her a precious encouragement, and the happiness he imparts will bring joy and peace to his own heart. (*Ministry of Healing,* page 374)

> "Marriage is the alliance of two people, one of whom never remembers birthdays and the other never forgets them."
>
> Ogden Nash

In life's toilsome way let the husband and father "lead on softly," as the companion of his journey is able to endure. Amidst the world's eager rush for wealth and power, let him learn to stay his steps, to comfort and support the one who is called to walk by his side. (*Ministry of Healing,* page 374)

> "A successful marriage requires falling in love many times, always with the same person."
>
> Mignon McLaughlin

Neither the husband nor the wife should attempt to exercise over the other an arbitrary control. Do not try to compel each other to yield to your wishes. You cannot do this and retain each other's love. Be kind, patient, and forbearing, considerate, and courteous. By the grace of God you can succeed in making each other happy, as in your marriage vow you promised to do. (*Ministry of Healing,* page 361)

Food for Thought

"My advice to you is to get married. If you find a good wife, you'll be happy; if not, you'll become a philosopher."

Socrates

Though difficulties, perplexities, and discouragements may arise, let neither husband nor wife harbor the thought that their union is a mistake or a disappointment. Determine to be all that it is possible to be to each other. Continue the early attentions. In every way encourage each other in fighting the battles of life. Study to advance the happiness of each other. Let there be mutual love, mutual forbearance. Then marriage, instead of being the end of love, will be as it were the very beginning of love. The warmth of true friendship, the love that binds heart to heart, is a foretaste of the joys of heaven. (*Ministry of Healing*, page 360)

"Many a man in love with a dimple makes the mistake of marrying the whole girl."

Stephen Leacock

Those who are contemplating marriage should consider what will be the character and influence of the home they are founding. As they become parents, a sacred trust is committed to them. Upon them depends in a great measure the well-being of their children in this world, and their happiness in the world to come. To a great extent they determine both the physical and the moral stamp that the little ones receive. And upon the character of the home depends the condition of society; the weight of each family's influence will tell in the upward or the downward scale. (*Ministry of Healing*, page 357)

Food for Thought

"Here's to matrimony, the high sea for which no compass has yet been invented!"

Heinrich Heine

Before assuming the responsibilities involved in marriage, young men and young women should have such an experience in practical life as will prepare them for its duties and its burdens. Early marriages are not to be encouraged. A relation so important as marriage and so far-reaching in its results should not be entered upon hastily, without sufficient preparation, and before the mental and physical powers are well developed. (*Ministry of Healing*, page 358)

"Don't smother each other. No one can grow in shade."

Leo Buscaglia

Let those who are contemplating marriage weigh every sentiment and watch every development of character in the one with whom they think to unite their life destiny. Let every step toward a marriage alliance be characterized by modesty, simplicity, sincerity, and an earnest purpose to please and honor God. Marriage affects the afterlife both in this world and in the world to come. A sincere Christian will make no plans that God cannot approve. (*Ministry of Healing*, page 359)

"Between friends differences in taste or opinion are irritating in direct proportion to their triviality."

W.H. Auden

Food for Thought

MEAT CONSUMPTION

Flesh was never the best food; but its use is now doubly objectionable, since disease in animals is so rapidly increasing. Those who use flesh foods little know what they are eating. Often if they could see the animals when living and know the quality of the meat they eat, they would turn from it with loathing. (*Ministry of Healing,* page 313)

> "I'm stopped. I'll never eat another burger."
>
> Oprah Winfrey

Upon their settlement in Canaan, the Israelites were permitted the use of animal food, but under careful restrictions which tended to lessen the evil results. The use of swine's flesh was prohibited, as also of other animals and of birds and fish whose flesh was pronounced unclean. Of the meats permitted, the eating of the fat and the blood was strictly forbidden. (*Ministry of Healing,* page 311)

> "I have been a vegetarian for a few years. Fred Dryer of the Rams has been one for ten years. It shows you don't need meat to play football."
>
> Joe Namath

In choosing man's food in Eden, the Lord showed what was the best diet; in the choice made for Israel He taught the same lesson. It was only because of their discontent and their murmuring for the fleshpots of Egypt that animal food was granted them, and this only for a short time. Its use brought disease and death to thousands. Yet the restriction to a non-flesh diet was never heartily accepted. (*Ministry of Healing,* page 311)

> "The beef industry has contributed to more American deaths than all the wars of this century, all natural disasters, and all automobile accidents combined. If beef is your idea of real food for real people, you'd better live real close to a real good hospital."
>
> Dr. Neal Barnard

Many who discard flesh meats and other gross and injurious articles think that because their food is simple and wholesome they may indulge appetite without restraint, and they eat to excess, sometimes to gluttony. This is an error. The digestive organs should not be burdened with a quantity or quality of food which it will tax the system to appropriate. (*Ministry of Healing*, page 306)

> "A man can live and be healthy without killing animals for food; therefore, if he eats meat, he participates in taking animal life merely for the sake of his appetite. And to act so is unmoral."
>
> Leo Tolstoy

When the use of flesh food is discontinued, there is often a sense of weakness, a lack of vigor. Many urge this as evidence that flesh food is essential; but it is because foods of this class are stimulating, because they fever the blood and excite the nerves, that they are so missed. Some will find it as difficult to leave off flesh eating as it is for the drunkard to give up his dram; but they will be the better for the change. (*Ministry of Healing*, page 316)

> "You have just dined, and however scrupulously the slaughterhouse is concealed in the graceful distance of miles, there is complicity."
>
> Ralph Waldo Emerson

By departing from the plan divinely appointed for their diet, the Israelites suffered great loss. They desired a flesh diet, and they

Food for Thought

reaped its results. They did not reach God's ideal of character or fulfill His purpose. The Lord "gave them their request; but sent leanness into their soul." Psalm 106:15. They valued the earthly above the spiritual, and the sacred pre-eminence which was His purpose for them they did not attain. (*Ministry of Healing*, page 312)

> "The practical objection to animal food in my case was its unseemliness; and, besides, when I had caught, and cleaned, and cooled, and eaten my fish, they seemed not to have fed me essentially. It was insignificant and unnecessary, and cost more than it came to. A little bread or a few potatoes would have done as well, with less trouble and filth."
>
> Henry David Thoreau

The diet appointed man in the beginning did not include animal food. Not till after the Flood, when every green thing on the earth had been destroyed, did man receive permission to eat flesh. (*Ministry of Healing*, page 311)

> "We consume the carcasses of creatures of like appetites, passions and organs with our own, and fill the slaughterhouses daily with screams of pain and fear."
>
> Robert Louis Stevenson

The tissues of the swine swarm with parasites. Of the swine God said, "It is unclean unto you: ye shall not eat of their flesh, nor touch their dead carcass." Deuteronomy 14:8. This command was given because swine's flesh is unfit for food. Swine are scavengers, and this is the only use they were intended to serve. Never, under any circumstances, was their flesh to be eaten by human beings. It is impossible for the flesh of any living creature to be wholesome when filth is its natural element and when it feeds upon every detestable thing. (*Ministry of Healing*, page 313)

Food for Thought

> "Vegetarianism is harmless enough though it is apt to fill a man with wind and self-righteousness."
>
> Robert Hutchison

The effects of a flesh diet may not be immediately realized; but this is no evidence that it is not harmful. Few can be made to believe that it is the meat they have eaten which has poisoned their blood and caused their suffering. Many die of diseases wholly due to meat eating, while the real cause is not suspected by themselves or by others. (*Ministry of Healing*, page 315)

> "To my mind, the life of a lamb is no less precious than that of a human being. I should be unwilling to take the life of a lamb for the sake of the human body."
>
> Mahatma Gandhi

Only such animals could be used for food as were in good condition. No creature that was torn, that had died of itself, or from which the blood had not been carefully drained, could be used as food. (*Ministry of Healing*, page 312)

> "Civilization . . . wrecks the planet from seafloor to stratosphere."
>
> Richard Bach

MEDICINE

By the use of poisonous drugs, many bring upon themselves lifelong illness, and many lives are lost that might be saved by

Food for Thought

the use of natural methods of healing. The poisons contained in many so-called remedies create habits and appetites that mean ruin to both soul and body. Many of the popular nostrums called patent medicines, and even some of the drugs dispensed by physicians, act a part in laying the foundation of the liquor habit, the opium habit, the morphine habit, that are so terrible a curse to society. (*Ministry of Healing,* page 126)

> "Nearly all men die of their medicines, not of their diseases."
>
> Moliére

People need to be taught that drugs do not cure disease. It is true that they sometimes afford present relief, and the patient appears to recover as the result of their use; this is because nature has sufficient vital force to expel the poison and to correct the conditions that caused the disease. Health is recovered in spite of the drug. But in most cases the drug only changes the form and location of the disease. Often the effect of the poison seems to be overcome for a time, but the results remain in the system and work great harm at some later period. (*Ministry of Healing,* page 126)

> "I firmly believe that if the entire materia medica as now used could be sunk to the bottom of the sea, it would be all the better for mankind—and all the worse for the fishes."
>
> Oliver Wendell Holmes, Sr.

Food for Thought

MENTAL FITNESS

Those who have broken down from mental labor should have rest from wearing thought; but they should not be led to believe that it is dangerous to use their mental powers at all. (*Ministry of Healing*, page 238)

> "It may be possible to incorporate laughter into daily activities, just as is done with other heart-healthy activities, such as taking the stairs instead of the elevator. The recommendation for a healthy heart may one day be exercise, eat right and laugh a few times a day."
>
> Dr. Michael Miller

The relation that exists between the mind and the body is very intimate. When one is affected, the other sympathizes. The condition of the mind affects the health to a far greater degree than many realize. Many of the diseases from which men suffer are the result of mental depression. Grief, anxiety, discontent, remorse, guilt, distrust, all tend to break down the life forces and to invite decay and death. (*Ministry of Healing*, page 241)

> "An imaginary ailment is worse than a disease."
>
> Hanan J. Ayalti

There is, however, a form of mind cure that is one of the most effective agencies for evil. Through this so-called science, one mind is brought under the control of another so that the individuality of the weaker is merged in that of the stronger mind. One person acts out the will of another. Thus it is claimed that the tenor of the thoughts may be changed, that health-giving impulses may be imparted, and patients may be

Food for Thought

enabled to resist and overcome disease. (*Ministry of Healing,* page 242)

> "We live longer than our forefathers; but we suffer more from a thousand artificial anxieties and cares. They fatigued only the muscles, we exhaust the finer strength of the nerves."
>
> Edward Bulwer-Lytton

Every day men in positions of trust have decisions to make upon which depend results of great importance. Often they have to think rapidly, and this can be done successfully by those only who practice strict temperance. The mind strengthens under the correct treatment of the physical and mental powers. If the strain is not too great, new vigor comes with every taxation. But often the work of those who have important plans to consider and important decisions to make is affected for evil by the results of improper diet. A disordered stomach produces a disordered, uncertain state of mind. Often it causes irritability, harshness, or injustice. Many a plan that would have been a blessing to the world has been set aside, many unjust, oppressive, even cruel measures have been carried, as the result of diseased conditions due to wrong habits of eating. (*Ministry of Healing,* page 309)

> "True silence is the rest of the mind; it is to the spirit what sleep is to the body, nourishment and refreshment."
>
> William Penn

The noise and excitement and confusion of the cities, their constrained and artificial life, are most wearisome and exhausting to the sick. The air, laden with smoke and dust, with poisonous gases, and with germs of disease, is a peril to life. The sick, for the most part shut within four walls, come almost to feel as if they were prisoners in their rooms. They look out on houses and pavements and hurrying crowds, with perhaps not even a glimpse of blue sky or sunshine, of grass or flower or tree. Shut up in this way, they brood over their suffering and sorrow and become a prey to their own sad thoughts. (*Ministry of Healing*, page 262)

> "Clarity of mind means clarity of passion, too; this is why a great and clear mind loves ardently and sees distinctly what it loves."
>
> Blaise Pascal

MONEY

Many despise economy, confounding it with stinginess and narrowness. But economy is consistent with the broadest liberality. Indeed, without economy, there can be no true liberality. We are to save, that we may give. (*Ministry of Healing*, page 206)

> "Thrift is not an affair of the pocket, but an affair of character."
>
> S.W. Straus

Money is a trust from God. It is not ours to expend for the gratification of pride or ambition. In the hands of God's children it is food for the hungry, and clothing for the naked. It is a defense to the oppressed, a means of health to the sick, a means of preaching the gospel to the poor. You could bring happiness to many hearts by using wisely the means that is now spent for show. (*Ministry of Healing*, page 287)

Food for Thought

"Money is the barometer of a society's virtue."

Ayn Rand

MORALITY BETWEEN PEERS

So frail, so ignorant, so liable to misconception is human nature, that each should be careful in the estimate he places upon another. We little know the bearing of our acts upon the experience of others. What we do or say may seem to us of little moment, when, could our eyes be opened, we should see that upon it depended the most important results for good or for evil. (*Ministry of Healing*, page 483)

"If you think about what you ought to do for other people, your character will take care of itself."

Woodrow Wilson

Our own homes and surroundings should be object lessons, teaching ways of improvement, so that industry, cleanliness, taste, and refinement may take the place of idleness, uncleanness, coarseness, and disorder. By our lives and example we can help others to discern that which is repulsive in their character or their surroundings, and with Christian courtesy we may encourage improvement. As we manifest an interest in them, we shall find opportunity to teach them how to put their energies to the best use. (*Ministry of Healing*, page 196)

"The first great gift we can bestow on others is a good example."

Thomas Morell

Food for Thought

$\mathcal{D}$o not retaliate. So far as you can do so, remove all cause for misapprehension. Avoid the appearance of evil. Do all that lies in your power, without the sacrifice of principle, to conciliate others. (*Ministry of Healing*, page 485)

> "Every one should consider himself as entrusted not only with his own conduct, but with that of others; and as accountable, not only for the duties which he neglects, or the crimes that he commits, but for that negligence and irregularity which he may encourage or inculcate. Every man, in whatever station, has, or endeavors to have his followers, admirers, and imitators, and has therefore the influence of his example to watch with care."
>
> Samuel Johnson

MORALITY IN MEDICINE

The true physician is an educator. He recognizes his responsibility, not only to the sick who are under his direct care, but also to the community in which he lives. He stands as a guardian of both physical and moral health. It is his endeavor not only to teach right methods for the treatment of the sick, but to encourage right habits of living, and to spread a knowledge of right principles. (*Ministry of Healing*, page 125)

> "Hygiene is the corruption of medicine by morality. It is impossible to find a hygienist who does not debase his theory of the healthful with a theory of the virtuous. The true aim of medicine is not to make men virtuous; it is to safeguard and rescue them from the consequences of their vices."
>
> H.L. Mencken

Food for Thought

The physician is continually brought into contact with those who need the strength and encouragement of a right example. Many are weak in moral power. They lack self-control and are easily overcome by temptation. The physician can help these souls only as he reveals in his own life a strength of principle that enables him to triumph over every injurious habit and defiling lust. In his life must be seen the working of a power that is divine. If he fails here, however forcible or persuasive his words may be, his influence will tell for evil. (*Ministry of Healing*, page 133)

> "The disease of an evil conscience is beyond the practice of all the physicians of all the countries in the world."
>
> William Gladstone

The physician's only safety is, under all circumstances, to act from principle, strengthened and ennobled by a firmness of purpose found only in God. He is to stand in the moral excellence of His character. Day by day, hour by hour, moment by moment, he is to live as in the sight of the unseen world. (*Ministry of Healing*, page 135)

> "The doctor may also learn more about the illness from the way the patient tells the story than from the story itself."
>
> Dr. James B. Herrick

MORALITY IN SELF

Always act from principle, never from impulse. Temper the natural impetuosity of your nature with meekness and gentleness.

Food for Thought

Indulge in no lightness or trifling. Let no low witticism escape your lips. Even the thoughts are not to be allowed to run riot. (*Ministry of Healing*, page 491)

> "We sometimes learn more from the sight of evil than from an example of good; and it is well to accustom ourselves to profit by the evil which is so common, while that which is good is so rare."
>
> Blaise Pascal

Life is chiefly made up, not of great sacrifices and wonderful achievements, but of little things. It is oftenest through the little things which seem so unworthy of notice that great good or evil is brought into our lives. It is through our failure to endure the tests that come to us in little things, that the habits are molded, the character misshaped; and when the greater tests come, they find us unready. Only by acting upon principle in the tests of daily life can we acquire power to stand firm and faithful in the most dangerous and most difficult positions. (*Ministry of Healing*, page 490)

> "Fullness of knowledge always means some understanding of the depths of our ignorance; and then is always conducive to humility and reverence."
>
> Robert Millikan

Remember that in whatever position you may serve you are revealing motive, developing character. Whatever your work, do it with exactness, with diligence; overcome the inclination to seek an easy task. (*Ministry of Healing*, page 499)

> One impulse from a vernal wood
> May teach you more of man,
> Of moral evil and of good,
> Than all the sages can.
>
> William Wordsworth

Food for Thought

Our time here is short. We can pass through this world but once; as we pass along, let us make the most of life. The work to which we are called does not require wealth or social position or great ability. It requires a kindly, self-sacrificing spirit and a steadfast purpose. A lamp, however small, if kept steadily burning, may be the means of lighting many other lamps. Our sphere of influence may seem narrow, our ability small, our opportunities few, our acquirements limited; yet wonderful possibilities are ours through a faithful use of the opportunities of our own homes. If we will open our hearts and homes to the divine principles of life we shall become channels for currents of life-giving power. (*Ministry of Healing*, page 355)

> "There are many people who reach their conclusions about life like schoolboys; they cheat their master by copying the answer out of a book without having worked out the sum for themselves."
>
> Søren Kierkegaard

No one should permit opposition or ridicule, or a desire to please or influence others, to turn him from true principles, or cause him lightly to regard them. Those who are governed by principle will be firm and decided in standing for the right. (*Ministry of Healing*, page 324)

> "Never let your sense of morals get in the way of doing what's right."
>
> Isaac Asimov

For those who do reform, how bitter the struggle to regain their manhood! And all their life long, in a shattered constitution, a wavering will, impaired intellect, and weakened soul power, many reap the harvest of their evil sowing. How much more might be accomplished if the evil were dealt with at the beginning! (*Ministry of Healing*, page 351)

Food for Thought

> "Moral codes adjust themselves to environmental conditions."
>
> William J. Durant

MORALITY IN SOCIETY

Governors, senators, representatives, judges, men who enact and administer a nation's laws, men who hold in their hands the lives, the fair fame, the possessions of their fellows, should be men of strict temperance. Only thus can their minds be clear to discriminate between right and wrong. Only thus can they possess firmness of principle, and wisdom to administer justice and to show mercy. But how does the record stand? (*Ministry of Healing*, page 345)

> "One who is injured ought not to return the injury, for on no account can it be right to do an injustice; and it is not right to return an injury, or to do evil to any man, however much we have suffered from him."
>
> Socrates

Many were forced to struggle with poverty and hardship. They early learned to work, and their active life in the open air gave vigor and elasticity to all their faculties. Forced to depend upon their own resources, they learned to combat difficulties and to surmount obstacles, and they gained courage and perseverance. They learned the lessons of self-reliance and self-control. Sheltered in a great degree from evil associations, they were satisfied with natural pleasures and wholesome companionships. They were simple in their tastes and temperate in their habits.

Food for Thought

They were governed by principle, and they grew up pure and strong and true. When called to their lifework, they brought to it physical and mental power, buoyancy of spirit, ability to plan and execute, and steadfastness in resisting evil, that made them a positive power for good in the world. (*Ministry of Healing*, page 366)

> "We are not naive enough to ask for pure men; we ask merely for men whose impurity does not conflict with the obligations of their job."
>
> Jean Rostand

The progress of reform depends upon a clear recognition of fundamental truth. While, on the one hand, danger lurks in a narrow philosophy and a hard, cold orthodoxy, on the other hand there is great danger in a careless liberalism. The foundation of all enduring reform is the law of God. We are to present in clear, distinct lines the need of obeying this law. Its principles must be kept before the people. They are as everlasting and inexorable as God Himself. (*Ministry of Healing*, page 129)

> "Non-violence leads to the highest ethics, which is the goal of all evolution. Until we stop harming all other living beings, we are still savages."
>
> Thomas Edison

In the warfare in which we are engaged, all may win who will discipline themselves by obedience to right principles. The practice of these principles in the details of life is too often looked upon as unimportant—a matter too trivial to demand attention. But in view of the issues at stake, nothing with which we have to do is small. Every act casts its weight into the scale that determines life's victory or defeat. (*Ministry of Healing*, page 129)

Food for Thought

"You have all the characteristics of a popular politician: a horrible voice, bad breeding, and a vulgar manner."

Aristophanes

*H*ow much more important is such carefulness to ensure success in the conflict of life. It is not mimic battles in which we are engaged. We are waging a warfare upon which hang eternal results. We have unseen enemies to meet. Evil angels are striving for the dominion of every human being. Whatever injures the health, not only lessens physical vigor, but tends to weaken the mental and moral powers. Indulgence in any unhealthful practice makes it more difficult for one to discriminate between right and wrong, and hence more difficult to resist evil. It increases the danger of failure and defeat. (*Ministry of Healing*, page 128)

"I still believe that one day mankind will bow before the altars of God and be crowned triumphant over war and bloodshed, and nonviolent redemptive goodwill will proclaim the rule of the land. Most of these people will never make the headlines and their names will not appear in Who's Who. Yet when years have rolled past and when the blazing light of truth is focused on this marvelous age in which we live—men and women will know and children will be taught that we have a finer land, a better people, a more noble civilization—because these humble children of God were willing to suffer for righteousness' sake."

Dr. Martin Luther King, Jr.

Food for Thought

MOTHER APPRECIATION

The mother's work often seems to her an unimportant service. It is a work that is rarely appreciated. Others know little of her many cares and burdens. Her days are occupied with a round of little duties, all calling for patient effort, for self-control, for tact, wisdom, and self-sacrificing love; yet she cannot boast of what she has done as any great achievement. She has only kept things in the home running smoothly; often weary and perplexed, she has tried to speak kindly to the children, to keep them busy and happy, and to guide the little feet in the right path. She feels that she has accomplished nothing. But it is not so. Heavenly angels watch the care-worn mother, noting the burdens she carries day by day. Her name may not have been heard in the world, but it is written in the Lamb's book of life. (*Ministry of Healing*, page 376)

> "Mother's love is peace. It need not be acquired, it need not be deserved."
>
> Erich Fromm

If the mother is deprived of the care and comforts she should have, if she is allowed to exhaust her strength through overwork or through anxiety and gloom, her children will be robbed of the vital force and of the mental elasticity and cheerful buoyancy they should inherit. Far better will it be to make the mother's life bright and cheerful, to shield her from want, wearing labor, and depressing care, and let the children inherit good constitutions, so that they may battle their way through life with their own energetic strength. (*Ministry of Healing*, page 375)

> "The strength of motherhood is greater than natural laws."
>
> Barbara Kingsolver

Food for Thought

*M*any advisers urge that every wish of the mother should be gratified; that if she desires any article of food, however harmful, she should freely indulge her appetite. Such advice is false and mischievous. The mother's physical needs should in no case be neglected. Two lives are depending upon her, and her wishes should be tenderly regarded, her needs generously supplied. But at this time above all others she should avoid, in diet and in every other line, whatever would lessen physical or mental strength. By the command of God Himself she is placed under the most solemn obligation to exercise self-control. (*Ministry of Healing*, page 373)

> "A mother is a person who seeing there are only four pieces of pie for five people, promptly announces she never did care for pie."
>
> Tenneva Jordan

*I*n many a home the wife and mother has no time to read, to keep herself well informed, no time to be a companion to her husband, no time to keep in touch with the developing minds of her children. Little by little she sinks into a mere household drudge, her strength and time and interest absorbed in the things that perish with the using. Too late she awakes to find herself almost a stranger in her own home. The precious opportunities once hers to influence her dear ones for the higher life, unimproved, have passed away forever. (*Ministry of Healing*, page 368)

> "Mother—that was the bank where we deposited all our hurts and worries."
>
> T. De Witt Talmage

*T*he strength of the mother should be tenderly cherished. (*Ministry of Healing*, page 373)

Food for Thought

"Being a full-time mother is one of the highest salaried jobs in my field, since the payment is pure love."

Mildred B. Vermont

MOTHERS AND CHILDREN

Young children love companionship and can seldom enjoy themselves alone. They yearn for sympathy and tenderness. That which they enjoy they think will please mother also, and it is natural for them to go to her with their little joys and sorrows. The mother should not wound their sensitive hearts by treating with indifference matters that, though trifling to her, are of great importance to them. Her sympathy and approval are precious. An approving glance, a word of encouragement or commendation, will be like sunshine in their hearts, often making the whole day happy. (*Ministry of Healing*, page 388)

"A mother is the truest friend we have, when trials, heavy and sudden, fall upon us; when adversity takes the place of prosperity; when friends who rejoice with us in our sunshine, desert us when troubles thicken around us, still will she cling to us, and endeavor by her kind precepts and counsels to dissipate the clouds of darkness, and cause peace to return to our hearts."

Washington Irving

By entering into their feelings and directing their amusements and employments, the mother will gain the confidence of her children, and she can then more effectually correct wrong habits, or check the manifestations of selfishness or passion. A word of caution or reproof spoken at the right time will be of great value. By patient, watchful love, she can turn the minds of the children

Food for Thought

in the right direction, cultivating in them beautiful and attractive traits of character. (*Ministry of Healing*, page 389)

> "A mother's love for her child is like nothing else in the world. It knows no law, no pity, it dares all things and crushes down remorselessly all that stands in its path."
>
> Agatha Christie

The more quiet and simple the life of the child, the more favorable it will be to both physical and mental development. At all times the mother should endeavor to be quiet, calm, and self-possessed. Many infants are extremely susceptible to nervous excitement, and the mother's gentle, unhurried manner will have a soothing influence that will be of untold benefit to the child. (*Ministry of Healing*, page 381)

> Youth fades; love droops; the leaves of friendship fall:
> A mother's secret hope outlives them all.
>
> Oliver Wendell Holmes, Sr.

Some mothers are not uniform in the treatment of their children. At times they indulge them to their injury, and again they refuse some innocent gratification that would make the childish heart very happy. (*Ministry of Healing*, page 390)

> "Grown don't mean nothing to a mother. A child is a child. They get bigger, older, but grown? What's that suppose to mean? In my heart it don't mean a thing."
>
> Toni Morrison

Food for Thought

Mothers who gratify the desires of their children at the expense of health and happy tempers, are sowing seeds of evil that will spring up and bear fruit. Self-indulgence grows with the growth of the little ones, and both mental and physical vigor are sacrificed. Mothers who do this work reap with bitterness the seed they have sown. They see their children grow up unfitted in mind and character to act a noble and useful part in society or in the home. The spiritual as well as the mental and physical powers suffer under the influence of unhealthful food. The conscience becomes stupefied, and the susceptibility to good impressions is impaired. (*Ministry of Healing,* page 384)

> "She never quite leaves her children at home, even when she doesn't take them along."
>
> Margaret Culkin Banning

MOTHERS' DUTIES

Many a widowed mother with her fatherless children is bravely striving to bear her double burden, often toiling far beyond her strength in order to keep her little ones with her and to provide for their needs. Little time has she for their training and instruction, little opportunity to surround them with influences that would brighten their lives. She needs encouragement, sympathy, and tangible help. (*Ministry of Healing,* page 203)

Food for Thought

> "Work is a responsibility most adults assume, a burden at times, a complication, but also a challenge that, like children, requires enormous energy and that holds the potential for qualitative, as well as quantitative, rewards. Isn't this the only constructive perspective for women who have no choice but to work? And isn't it a more healthy attitude for women writhing with guilt because they choose to compound the challenges of motherhood with work they enjoy?"
>
> Melinda M. Marshall

The mother who appreciates this will regard her opportunities as priceless. Earnestly will she seek, in her own character and by her methods of training, to present before her children the highest ideal. Earnestly, patiently, courageously, she will endeavor to improve her own abilities, that she may use aright the highest powers of the mind in the training of her children. Earnestly will she inquire at every step, "What hath God spoken?" Diligently she will study His word. She will keep her eyes fixed upon Christ, that her own daily experience, in the lowly round of care and duty, may be a true reflection of the one true Life. (*Ministry of Healing,* page 378)

> "The good mother knows that frustration teaches tolerance and that instant gratification is not always best; the too good mother meets all of her son's needs instantly. The good enough mother knows that a son needs to have ownership of his actions. She stands on the sidelines and cheers him on but lets him run past her in the race. The too good mother keeps her child from becoming independent; she mothers in a way that benefits herself, not her son."
>
> Elyse Zorn Karlin

The mother should cultivate a cheerful, contented, happy disposition. Every effort in this direction will be abundantly

Food for Thought

repaid in both the physical well-being and the moral character of her children. A cheerful spirit will promote the happiness of her family and in a very great degree improve her own health. (*Ministry of Healing*, page 374)

> "Most of all the other beautiful things in life come by twos and threes, by dozens and hundreds. Plenty of roses, stars, sunsets, rainbows, brothers and sisters, aunts and cousins, comrades and friends—but only one mother in the whole world."
>
> Kate Douglas Wiggin

There is work for mothers in helping their children to form correct habits and pure tastes. Educate the appetite; teach the children to abhor stimulants. Bring your children up to have moral stamina to resist the evil that surrounds them. Teach them that they are not to be swayed by others, that they are not to yield to strong influences, but to influence others for good. (*Ministry of Healing*, page 334)

> "A mother's happiness is like a beacon, lighting up the future but reflected also on the past in the guise of fond memories."
>
> Honoré de Balzac

The mother who permits her child to be nourished by another should consider well what the result may be. (*Ministry of Healing*, page 383)

> "A pair of substantial mammary glands has the advantage over the two hemispheres of the most learned professor's brain, in the art of compounding a nutritious fluid for infants."
>
> Oliver Wendell Holmes, Sr.

Food for Thought

The best food for the infant is the food that nature provides. Of this it should not be needlessly deprived. It is a heartless thing for a mother, for the sake of convenience or social enjoyment, to seek to free herself from the tender office of nursing her little one. (*Ministry of Healing,* page 383)

> "Sweater, n.: garment worn by child when its mother is feeling chilly."
> — Ambrose Bierce

For lack of time and thought, many a mother refuses her children some innocent pleasure, while busy fingers and weary eyes are diligently engaged on work designed only for adornment, something that, at best, will serve only to encourage vanity and extravagance in their young hearts. As the children approach manhood and womanhood, these lessons bear fruit in pride and moral worthlessness. The mother grieves over her children's faults, but does not realize that the harvest she is reaping is from seed which she herself planted. (*Ministry of Healing,* page 389)

> "Making the decision to have a child is momentous. It is to decide forever to have your heart go walking around outside your body."
> — Elizabeth Stone

The well-being of the child will be affected by the habits of the mother. Her appetites and passions are to be controlled by principle. There is something for her to shun, something for her to work against, if she fulfills God's purpose for her in giving her a child. If before the birth of her child she is self-indulgent, if she is selfish, impatient, and exacting, these traits will be reflected in the disposition of the child. Thus many children have

received as a birthright almost unconquerable tendencies to evil.
(*Ministry of Healing*, page 372)

> "Cleaning your house while your kids are still growing up is like shoveling the walk before it stops snowing."
>
> Phyllis Diller

Especially does responsibility rest upon the mother. She, by whose lifeblood the child is nourished and its physical frame built up, imparts to it also mental and spiritual influences that tend to the shaping of mind and character. It was Jochebed, the Hebrew mother, who, strong in faith, was 'not afraid of the king's commandment' (Hebrews 11:23), of whom was born Moses, the deliverer of Israel. It was Hannah, the woman of prayer and self-sacrifice and heavenly inspiration, who gave birth to Samuel, the heaven-instructed child, the incorruptible judge, the founder of Israel's sacred schools. It was Elizabeth the kinswoman and kindred spirit of Mary of Nazareth, who was the mother of the Saviour's herald. (*Ministry of Healing*, page 372)

> "There's nothing that can help you understand your beliefs more than trying to explain them to an inquisitive child."
>
> Frank A. Clark

No other work can equal hers in importance. She has not, like the artist, to paint a form of beauty upon canvas, nor, like the sculptor, to chisel it from marble. She has not, like the author, to embody a noble thought in words of power, nor, like the musician, to express a beautiful sentiment in melody. It is hers, with the help of God, to develop in a human soul the likeness of the divine. (*Ministry of Healing*, page 377)

Food for Thought

"Some are kissing mothers and some are scolding mothers, but it is love just the same."

Pearl S. Buck

All parents have it in their power to learn much concerning the care and prevention, and even the treatment, of disease. Especially ought the mother to know what to do in common cases of illness in her family. She should know how to minister to her sick child. Her love and insight should fit her to perform services for it which could not so well be trusted to a stranger's hand. (*Ministry of Healing*, page 385)

"If evolution really works, how come mothers only have two hands?"

Milton Berle

NATURE

Nature's abundant supply of fruits, nuts, and grains is ample, and year by year the products of all lands are more generally distributed to all, by the increased facilities for transportation. As a result many articles of food which a few years ago were regarded as expensive luxuries are now within the reach of all as foods for everyday use. This is especially the case with dried and canned fruits. (*Ministry of Healing*, page 297)

Food for Thought

"Climb the mountains and get their good tidings. Nature's peace will flow into you as sunshine flows into trees. The winds will blow their freshness into you, and the storms their energy, while cares will drop off like falling leaves."

John Muir

It was not God's purpose that people should be crowded into cities, huddled together in terraces and tenements. In the beginning He placed our first parents amidst the beautiful sights and sounds He desires us to rejoice in today. The more nearly we come into harmony with God's original plan, the more favorable will be our position to secure health of body, and mind, and soul. (*Ministry of Healing*, page 365)

"Beauty is an ecstasy; it is as simple as hunger. There is really nothing to be said about it. It is like the perfume of a rose: you can smell it and that is all."

W. Somerset Maugham

Trees that are crowded closely together do not grow healthfully and sturdily. The gardener transplants them that they may have room to develop. (*Ministry of Healing*, page 152)

"To find the universal elements enough; to find the air and the water exhilarating; to be refreshed by a morning walk or an evening saunter; to be thrilled by the stars at night; to be elated over a bird's nest or a wildflower in spring—these are some of the rewards of the simple life."

John Burroughs

The Creator chose for our first parents the surroundings best adapted for their health and happiness. He did not place them in a palace or surround them with the artificial adornments and luxuries that so many today are struggling to obtain. He placed

Food for Thought

them in close touch with nature and in close communion with the holy ones of heaven. (*Ministry of Healing,* page 261)

> "The love of wilderness is more than a hunger for what is always beyond reach; it is also an expression of loyalty to the earth, the earth which bore us and sustains us, the only paradise we shall ever know, the only paradise we ever need—if only we had the eyes to see . . . No, wilderness is not a luxury but a necessity of the human spirit, as vital to our lives as water and good bread."
>
> Edward Abbey

In the garden that God prepared as a home for His children, graceful shrubs and delicate flowers greeted the eye at every turn. There were trees of every variety, many of them laden with fragrant and delicious fruit. On their branches the birds caroled their songs of praise. Under their shadow the creatures of the earth sported together without a fear. (*Ministry of Healing,* page 261)

> "There is no other door to knowledge than the door Nature opens; and there is no truth except the truths we discover in Nature."
>
> Luther Burbank

Wherever fruit can be grown in abundance, a liberal supply should be prepared for winter, by canning or drying. Small fruits, such as currants, gooseberries, strawberries, raspberries, and blackberries, can be grown to advantage in many places where they are but little used and their cultivation is neglected. (*Ministry of Healing,* page 299)

> "The Amen of nature is always a flower."
>
> Oliver Wendell Holmes, Sr.

Food for Thought

Adam and Eve, in their untainted purity, delighted in the sights and sounds of Eden. God appointed them their work in the garden, "to dress it and to keep it." Genesis 2:15. Each day's labor brought them health and gladness, and the happy pair greeted with joy the visits of their Creator, as in the cool of the day He walked and talked with them. Daily God taught them His lessons. (*Ministry of Healing*, page 261)

> "Earth is here so kind, that just tickle her with a hoe and she laughs with a harvest."
>
> Douglas William Jerrold

Cut off to a great degree from contact with and dependence upon men, and separated from the world's corrupting maxims and customs and excitements, they would come nearer to the heart of nature. God's presence would be more real to them. Many would learn the lesson of dependence upon Him. Through nature they would hear His voice speaking to their hearts of His peace and love, and mind and soul and body would respond to the healing, life-giving power. (*Ministry of Healing*, page 192)

> "I smelt the violets in her hand and asked, half in words, half in signs, a question which meant, is love the sweetness of flowers?"
>
> Helen Keller

How glad would they be to sit in the open air, rejoice in the sunshine, and breathe the fragrance of tree and flower! There are life-giving properties in the balsam of the pine, in the fragrance of the cedar and the fir, and other trees also have properties that are health restoring. (*Ministry of Healing*, page 264)

Food for Thought

> "The air, the water and the ground are free gifts to man and no one has the power to portion them out in parcels. Man must drink and breathe and walk and therefore each man has a right to his share of each."
>
> James Fenimore Cooper

NURSES

An important part of the nurse's duty is the care of the patient's diet. The patient should not be allowed to suffer or become unduly weakened through lack of nourishment, nor should the enfeebled digestive powers be overtaxed. Care should be taken so to prepare and serve the food that it will be palatable, but wise judgment should be used in adapting it to the needs of the patient, both in quantity and quality. In times of convalescence especially, when the appetite is keen, before the digestive organs have recovered strength, there is great danger of injury from errors in diet. (*Ministry of Healing*, page 221)

> "Constant attention by a good nurse may be just as important as a major operation by a surgeon."
>
> Dag Hammarskjöld

The efficiency of the nurse depends, to a great degree, upon physical vigor. The better the health, the better will she be able to endure the strain of attendance upon the sick, and the more successfully can she perform her duties. Those who care for the sick should give special attention to diet, cleanliness, fresh air, and exercise. Like carefulness on the part of the family will enable them also to endure the extra burdens brought upon

them, and will help to prevent them from contracting disease.
(*Ministry of Healing,* page 219)

> "No man, not even a doctor, ever gives any other definition of what a nurse should be than this—'devoted and obedient.' This definition would do just as well for a porter. It might even do for a horse. It would not do for a policeman."
>
> Florence Nightingale

OPTIMISM

Under such influences as these, many suffering ones will be guided into the way of life. Angels of heaven cooperate with human instrumentalities in bringing encouragement and hope and joy and peace to the hearts of the sick and suffering. Under such conditions the sick are doubly blessed, and many find health. The feeble step recovers its elasticity. The eye regains its brightness. The hopeless become hopeful. The once despondent countenance wears an expression of joy. The complaining tones of the voice give place to tones of cheerfulness and content.
(*Ministry of Healing,* page 267)

> "Underlying the whole scheme of civilization is the confidence men have in each other, confidence in their integrity, confidence in their honesty, confidence in their future."
>
> W. Bourke Cockran

Men of stamina are wanted, men who will not wait to have their way smoothed and every obstacle removed, men who will inspire with fresh zeal the flagging efforts of dispirited workers, men whose hearts are warm with Christian love and whose hands are strong to do their Master's work. (*Ministry of Healing*, page 497)

> "Fortune leaves always some door open to come at a remedy."
> — Miguel de Cervantes

In the future life the mysteries that here have annoyed and disappointed us will be made plain. We shall see that our seemingly unanswered prayers and disappointed hopes have been among our greatest blessings. (*Ministry of Healing*, page 474)

> "The optimist proclaims that we live in the best of all possible worlds; and the pessimist fears this is true."
> — James Branch Cabell

Cultivate the habit of speaking well of others. Dwell upon the good qualities of those with whom you associate, and see as little as possible of their errors and failings. When tempted to complain of what someone has said or done, praise something in that person's life or character. Cultivate thankfulness. It never pays to think of our grievances. (*Ministry of Healing*, page 492)

> "Technique and ability alone do not get you to the top; it is the willpower that is the most important. This willpower you cannot buy with money or be given by others . . . it rises from your heart"
> — Junko Tabei

"A merry [rejoicing] heart doeth good like a medicine." Proverbs 17:22. Gratitude, rejoicing, benevolence, trust in God's love and care—these are health's greatest safeguard. To the Israelites

Food for Thought

they were to be the very keynote of life. (*Ministry of Healing*, page 281)

> "I have been reading the morning paper. I do it every morning—knowing well that I shall find in it the usual depravities and basenesses and hypocrisies and cruelties that make up civilization, and cause me to put in the rest of the day pleading for the damnation of the human race. I cannot seem to get my prayers answered, yet I do not despair."
>
> Mark Twain

Express gratitude for the blessings you have; show appreciation of the attentions you receive. Keep the heart full of the precious promises of God, that you may bring forth from this treasure, words that will be a comfort and strength to others. This will surround you with an atmosphere that will be helpful and uplifting. Let it be your aim to bless those around you, and you will find ways of being helpful, both to the members of your own family and to others. (*Ministry of Healing*, page 257)

> "When you reach for the stars, you may not quite get them, but you won't come up with a handful of mud, either."
>
> Leo Burnett

When someone asks how you are feeling, do not try to think of something mournful to tell in order to gain sympathy. Do not talk of your lack of faith and your sorrows and sufferings. The tempter delights to hear such words. When talking on gloomy subjects, you are glorifying him. We are not to dwell on the great power of Satan to overcome us. Often we give ourselves into his hands by talking of his power. Let us talk instead of the great power of God to bind up all our interests with His own. Tell of the matchless power of Christ, and speak of His glory. All heaven

Food for Thought

is interested in our salvation. The angels of God, thousands upon thousands, and ten thousand times ten thousand, are commissioned to minister to those who shall be heirs of salvation. They guard us against evil and press back the powers of darkness that are seeking our destruction. Have we not reason to be thankful every moment, thankful even when there are apparent difficulties in our pathway? (*Ministry of Healing*, page 253)

> "There are two days in the week about which and upon which I never worry. Two carefree days, kept sacredly free from fear and apprehension. One of these days Is Yesterday . . . And the other . . . is Tomorrow."
>
> Robert Jones Burdette

PARENTING ADVICE

But, fathers, do not discourage your children. Combine affection with authority, kindness and sympathy with firm restraint. Give some of your leisure hours to your children; become acquainted with them; associate with them in their work and in their sports, and win their confidence. Cultivate friendship with them, especially with your sons. In this way you will be a strong influence for good. (*Ministry of Healing*, page 391)

> "Of course children benefit from positive feedback. But praise and rewards are not the only methods of reinforcement. More emphasis should be place on appreciation—reinforcement related explicitly and directly to the content of the child's interest and efforts."
>
> Lilian G. Katz

Food for Thought

𝒫arents, let the sunshine of love, cheerfulness, and happy contentment enter your own hearts, and let its sweet, cheering influence pervade your home. Manifest a kindly, forbearing spirit; and encourage the same in your children, cultivating all the graces that will brighten the home life. The atmosphere thus created will be to the children what air and sunshine are to the vegetable world, promoting health and vigor of mind and body. (*Ministry of Healing*, page 387)

> "Think of the child's question as the start of a two-way conversation rather than a question-and-answer session. Sometimes it may be necessary to learn what children think about the subject and what misconceptions they may have before providing an answer."
>
> Ruth Formanek

𝒯his work rests, in a great degree, with parents. In the efforts put forth to stay the progress of intemperance and of other evils that are eating like a cancer in the social body, if more attention were given to teaching parents how to form the habits and character of their children, a hundredfold more good would result. Habit, which is so terrible a force for evil, it is in their power to make a force for good. They have to do with the stream at its source, and it rests with them to direct it rightly. (*Ministry of Healing*, page 352)

> "I looked on child rearing not only as a work of love and duty but as a profession that was fully interesting and challenging as any honorable profession in the world and one that demanded the best that I could bring to it."
>
> Rose Kennedy

Food for Thought

Fathers and mothers need to understand their responsibility. The world is full of snares for the feet of the young. Multitudes are attracted by a life of selfish and sensual pleasure. They cannot discern the hidden dangers or the fearful ending of the path that seems to them the way of happiness. Through the indulgence of appetite and passion, their energies are wasted, and millions are ruined for this world and for the world to come. Parents should remember that their children must encounter these temptations. Even before the birth of the child, the preparation should begin that will enable it to fight successfully the battle against evil. (*Ministry of Healing,* page 371)

> "The quality of a civilization may be measured by how it cares for its elderly. Just as surely, the future of a society may be forecast by how it cares for its young."
>
> Daniel Patrick Moynihan

The father should do his part toward making home happy. Whatever his cares and business perplexities, they should not be permitted to overshadow his family; he should enter his home with smiles and pleasant words. (*Ministry of Healing,* page 392)

> "Children require guidance and sympathy far more than instruction."
>
> Anne Sullivan

The father should enforce in his family the sterner virtues—energy, integrity, honesty, patience, courage, diligence, and practical usefulness. And what he requires of his children he himself should practice, illustrating these virtues in his own manly bearing. (*Ministry of Healing,* page 391)

Food for Thought

"There are two great injustices that can befall a child. One is to punish him for something he didn't do. The other is to let him get away with doing something he knows is wrong."

Robert Gardner

PARENTING WISDOM

𝒫arents should live more for their children, and less for society. Study health subjects, and put your knowledge to a practical use. Teach your children to reason from cause to effect. Teach them that if they desire health and happiness, they must obey the laws of nature. Though you may not see so rapid improvement as you desire, be not discouraged, but patiently and perseveringly continue your work. (*Ministry of Healing*, page 386)

"It is easy to lose confidence in our natural ability to raise children. The true techniques for raising children are simple: Be with them, play with them, talk to them. You are not squandering their time no matter what the latest child development books say about purposeful play and cognitive learning skills."

Neil Kurshan

𝒩ot only the habits of the mother, but the training of the child were included in the angel's instruction to the Hebrew parents. It was not enough that Samson, the child who was to deliver Israel, should have a good legacy at his birth. This was to be followed by careful training. From infancy he was to be trained to habits of strict temperance. (*Ministry of Healing*, page 379)

Food for Thought

"We sometimes think that if we treat each child fairly and equally—and make them see that we're being fair—they will stop arguing about who gets more, who gets something first, who's our favorite. But as hard as we try to be fair, we can never succeed. Even if we believe we're completely fair, children will never agree with us. Since no one wins the fairness game, the best thing to do is avoid playing it."

Nancy Samalin

The nobler the aims, the higher the mental and spiritual endowments, and the better developed the physical powers of the parents, the better will be the life equipment they give their children. In cultivating that which is best in themselves, parents are exerting an influence to mold society and to uplift future generations. (*Ministry of Healing*, page 371)

"Children have never been very good at listening to their elders, but they have never failed to imitate them."

James Baldwin

Great is the honor and the responsibility placed upon fathers and mothers, in that they are to stand in the place of God to their children. Their character, their daily life, their methods of training, will interpret His words to the little ones. Their influence will win or repel the child's confidence in the Lord's assurances. (*Ministry of Healing*, page 375)

"The child is father of the man."

William Wordsworth

It is by the youth and children of today that the future of society is to be determined, and what these youth and children shall be depends upon the home. To the lack of right home training may

Food for Thought

be traced the larger share of the disease and misery and crime that curse humanity. If the home life were pure and true, if the children who went forth from its care were prepared to meet life's responsibilities and dangers, what a change would be seen in the world! (*Ministry of Healing*, page 351)

> "You can learn many things from children. How much patience you have, for instance."
>
> Franklin P. Jones

Parents may lay for their children the foundation for a healthy, happy life. They may send them forth from their homes with moral stamina to resist temptation, and courage and strength to wrestle successfully with life's problems. They may inspire in them the purpose and develop the power to make their lives an honor to God and a blessing to the world. (*Ministry of Healing*, page 352)

> "Children are living jewels dropped unsustained from heaven."
>
> Robert Pollok

Mothers should guard against training their children to be dependent and self-absorbed. Never lead them to think that they are the center, and that everything must revolve around them. Some parents give much time and attention to amusing their children, but children should be trained to amuse themselves, to exercise their own ingenuity and skill. Thus they will learn to be content with very simple pleasures. They should be taught to bear bravely their little disappointments and trials. Instead of calling attention to every trifling pain or hurt, divert their minds, teach them to pass lightly over little annoyances or discomforts. Study to suggest ways by which the children may learn to be thoughtful for others. (*Ministry of Healing*, page 389)

> "Good, honest, hardheaded character is a function of the home. If the proper seed is sown there and properly nourished for a few years, it will not be easy for that plant to be uprooted."
>
> George A. Dorsey

PARENTS TEACHING KIDS

If parents could be led to trace the result of their action, and could see how, by their example and teaching, they perpetuate and increase the power of sin or the power of righteousness, a change would certainly be made. Many would turn away from tradition and custom, and accept the divine principles of life. (*Ministry of Healing*, page 131)

> "Babies learn most of what they know from interactions with their parents, but not of the formal, instructional variety. Babies learn from spontaneous, everyday events—the mailman at the door with a package to open . . . all of which need adult interpretation. They are real events of interest and concern to babies and young children . . . By contrast, infant education is artificial and out of context."
>
> Sandra Scarr

Too much importance cannot be placed upon the early training of children. The lessons learned, the habits formed, during the years of infancy and childhood, have more to do with the formation of the character and the direction of the life than have all the instruction and training of after years. (*Ministry of Healing,* page 380)

> "Our first line of defense in raising children with values is modeling good behavior ourselves. This is critical. How will our kids learn tolerance for others if our hearts are filled with hate? Learn compassion if we are indifferent? Perceive academics as important if soccer practice is a higher priority than homework?"
>
> Fred G. Gosman

As children emerge from babyhood, great care should still be taken in educating their tastes and appetite. Often they are permitted to eat what they choose and when they choose, without reference to health. The pains and money so often lavished upon unwholesome dainties lead the young to think that the highest object in life, and that which yields the greatest amount of happiness, is to be able to indulge the appetite. The result of this training is gluttony, then comes sickness, which is usually followed by dosing with poisonous drugs. (*Ministry of Healing,* page 384)

> "Role modeling is the most basic responsibility of parents. Parents are handing life's scripts to their children, scripts that in all likelihood will be acted out for the rest of the children's lives."
>
> Stephen R. Covey

Teach your children from the cradle to practice self-denial and self-control. Teach them to enjoy the beauties of nature and in useful employments to exercise systematically all the powers of body and mind. Bring them up to have sound constitutions and good morals, to have sunny dispositions and sweet tempers. Impress upon their tender minds the truth that God does not design that we should live for present gratification merely, but for our ultimate good. Teach them that to yield to temptation is weak and wicked; to resist, noble and manly. These lessons will be as seed sown in good soil, and they will bear fruit that will make your hearts glad. (*Ministry of Healing,* page 386)

"One good mother is worth a hundred schoolmasters."

George Herbert

PESSIMISM

Those professed Christians who are constantly complaining, and who seem to think cheerfulness and happiness a sin, have not genuine religion. Those who take a mournful pleasure in all that is melancholy in the natural world, who choose to look upon dead leaves rather than to gather the beautiful living flowers, who see no beauty in grand mountain heights and in valleys clothed with living green, who close their senses to the joyful voice which speaks to them in nature, and which is sweet and musical to the listening ear—these are not in Christ. They are gathering to themselves gloom and darkness, when they might have brightness, even the Sun of Righteousness arising in their hearts with healing in His beams. (*Ministry of Healing,* page 251)

"The chemistry of dissatisfaction is as the chemistry of some marvelously potent tar. In it are the building stones of explosives, stimulants, poisons, opiates, perfumes, and stenches."

Eric Hoffer

Food for Thought

*I*f you do not feel lighthearted and joyous, do not talk of your feelings. Cast no shadow upon the lives of others. (*Ministry of Healing*, page 488)

> "There will always be dissident voices heard in the land, expressing opposition without alternatives, finding fault but never favor, perceiving gloom on every side and seeking influence without responsibility. Those voices are inevitable."
>
> John F. Kennedy

*W*hen people have nothing to occupy their time and attention, their thoughts become centered upon themselves, and they grow morbid and irritable. Many times they dwell upon their bad feelings until they think themselves much worse than they really are and wholly unable to do anything. (*Ministry of Healing*, page 239)

> "A sneer is the weapon of the weak."
>
> James Russell Lowell

*M*any are dissatisfied with their lifework. It may be that their surroundings are uncongenial; their time is occupied with commonplace work, when they think themselves capable of higher responsibilities; often their efforts seem to them to be unappreciated or fruitless; their future is uncertain. (*Ministry of Healing*, page 472)

> "The fault-finder will find faults even in paradise."
>
> Henry David Thoreau

*E*arnest workers have no time for dwelling upon the faults of others. We cannot afford to live on the husks of others' faults or failings. Evil-speaking is a twofold curse, falling more heavily upon the speaker than upon the hearer. He who scatters the seeds of dissension and strife reaps in his own soul the deadly fruits. The very act of looking for evil in others develops evil in those who look. By dwelling upon the faults of others, we are changed into the same image. (*Ministry of Healing*, page 492)

> "An age is called Dark, not because the light fails to shine, but because people refuse to see it."
>
> James Michener

Disease is sometimes produced, and is often greatly aggravated, by the imagination. Many are lifelong invalids who might be well if they only thought so. Many imagine that every slight exposure will cause illness, and the evil effect is produced because it is expected. Many die from disease the cause of which is wholly imaginary. (*Ministry of Healing*, page 241)

> "No one can cheat you out of ultimate success but yourself."
>
> Ralph Waldo Emerson

We need not keep our own record of trials and difficulties, griefs, and sorrows. All these things are written in the books, and heaven will take care of them. While we are counting up the disagreeable things, many things that are pleasant to reflect upon are passing from memory. (*Ministry of Healing*, page 487)

> "Gloom and solemnity are entirely out of place in even the most rigorous study of an art originally intended to make glad the heart of man."
>
> Ezra Pound

Food for Thought

*M*any seek medical advice and treatment who have become moral wrecks through their own wrong habits. They are bruised and weak and wounded, feeling their folly and their inability to overcome. Such ones should have nothing in their surroundings to encourage a continuance of the thoughts and feelings that have made them what they are. They need to breathe an atmosphere of purity, of high and noble thought. How terrible the responsibility when those who should give them a right example are themselves enthralled by hurtful habits, their influence affording to temptation an added strength! (*Ministry of Healing*, page 133)

"Some men see things as they are and ask why. Others dream things that never were and ask why not."

George Bernard Shaw

*W*e need to beware of self-pity. Never indulge the feeling that you are not esteemed as you should be, that your efforts are not appreciated, that your work is too difficult. (*Ministry of Healing*, page 476)

"A little neglect may breed mischief: for want of a nail the shoe was lost; for want of a shoe the horse was lost; and for want of a horse the rider was lost."

Benjamin Franklin

*T*here are many whose hearts are aching under a load of care because they seek to reach the world's standard. They have chosen its service, accepted its perplexities, adopted its customs. Thus their character is marred and their life made a weariness. The continual worry is wearing out the life forces. (*Ministry of Healing*, page 481)

Food for Thought

"A pessimist sees only the dark side of the clouds, and mopes; a philosopher sees both sides, and shrugs; an optimist doesn't see the clouds at all—he's walking on them."

Leonard Louis Levinson

SEIZE THE DAY

Man can shape circumstances, but circumstances should not be allowed to shape the man. We should seize upon circumstances as instruments by which to work. We are to master them, but should not permit them to master us. (*Ministry of Healing,* page 500)

> "The best things in life are nearest: Breath in your nostrils, light in your eyes, flowers at your feet, duties at your hand, the path of right just before you. Then do not grasp at the stars, but do life's plain, common work as it comes, certain that daily duties and daily bread are the sweetest things in life."
>
> Robert Louis Stevenson

Life is mysterious and sacred. Precious are its opportunities, and earnestly should they be improved. Once lost, they are gone forever. (*Ministry of Healing,* page 397)

> "The soul should always stand ajar. Ready to welcome the ecstatic experience."
>
> Emily Dickinson

Multitudes long for a better life, but they lack courage and resolution to break away from the power of habit. They shrink

Food for Thought

from the effort and struggle and sacrifice demanded, and their lives are wrecked and ruined. Thus even men of the brightest minds, men of high aspirations and noble powers, otherwise fitted by nature and education to fill positions of trust and responsibility, are degraded and lost for this life and for the life to come. (*Ministry of Healing,* page 351)

> "What's really important in life? Sitting on a beach? Looking at television eight hours a day? I think we have to appreciate that we're alive for only a limited period of time, and we'll spend most of our lives working. That being the case, I believe one of the most important priorities is to do whatever we do as well as we can. We should take pride in that."
>
> — Victor Kiam

Wrongs cannot be righted, nor can reformations in conduct be made by a few feeble, intermittent efforts. Character building is the work, not of a day, nor of a year, but of a lifetime. The struggle for conquest over self, for holiness and heaven, is a lifelong struggle. Without continual effort and constant activity, there can be no advancement in the divine life, no attainment of the victor's crown. (*Ministry of Healing,* page 452)

> "Lost, yesterday, somewhere between sunrise and sunset, two golden hours, each set with sixty diamond minutes. No reward is offered for they are gone forever."
>
> — Horace Mann

The faithful discharge of today's duties is the best preparation for tomorrow's trials. Do not gather together all tomorrow's liabilities and cares and add them to the burden of today. (*Ministry of Healing,* page 481)

Food for Thought

> "To live content with small means; to seek elegance rather than luxury, and refinement rather than fashion; to be worthy, not respectable, and wealthy, not rich; to listen to stars and birds, babes and sages, with open heart; to study hard; to think quietly, act frankly, talk gently, await occasions, hurry never; in a word, to let the spiritual, unbidden and unconscious, grow up through the common—this is my symphony."
>
> — William Henry Channing

It is wrong to waste our time, wrong to waste our thoughts. We lose every moment that we devote to self-seeking. If every moment were valued and rightly employed, we should have time for everything that we need to do for ourselves or for the world. (*Ministry of Healing*, page 208)

> "Ideals are like stars; you will not succeed in touching them with your hands. But like the seafaring man on the desert of waters, you will choose them as your guide, and following them you will reach your destiny."
>
> — Carl Schurz

SELF-HEALING

In the battle with disease and death every energy is taxed to the limit of endurance. The reaction from this terrible strain tests the character to the utmost. Then it is that temptation has greatest power. More than men in any other calling, is the physician in need of self-control, purity of spirit, and that faith which takes hold on heaven. For the sake of others and for his own sake, he cannot afford to disregard physical law. Recklessness

Food for Thought

in physical habits tends to recklessness in morals. (*Ministry of Healing*, page 135)

> "We do not believe in ourselves until someone reveals that deep inside us is valuable, worth listening to, worthy of our trust, sacred to our touch. Once we believe in ourselves we can risk curiosity, wonder, spontaneous delight or any experience that reveals the human spirit."
>
> e.e. cummings

The power of the will is not valued as it should be. Let the will be kept awake and rightly directed, and it will impart energy to the whole being and will be a wonderful aid in the maintenance of health. It is a power also in dealing with disease. Exercised in the right direction, it would control the imagination and be a potent means of resisting and overcoming disease of both mind and body. By the exercise of the willpower in placing themselves in right relation to life, patients can do much to cooperate with the physician's efforts for their recovery. There are thousands who can recover health if they will. The Lord does not want them to be sick. He desires them to be well and happy, and they should make up their minds to be well. Often invalids can resist disease simply by refusing to yield to ailments and settle in a state of inactivity. Rising above their aches and pains, let them engage in useful employment suited to their strength. By such employment and the free use of air and sunlight, many an emaciated invalid might recover health and strength. (*Ministry of Healing*, page 246)

> "What lies behind us and what lies before us are tiny matters compared to what lies within us."
>
> Ralph Waldo Emerson

Food for Thought

SPENDING EXTRAVAGANTLY

Many a woman, forced to prepare for herself or her children the stylish costumes demanded by fashion, is doomed to ceaseless drudgery. Many a mother with throbbing nerves and trembling fingers toils far into the night to add to her children's clothing ornamentation that contributes nothing to healthfulness, comfort, or real beauty. For the sake of fashion she sacrifices health and that calmness of spirit so essential to the right guidance of her children. The culture of mind and heart is neglected. The soul is dwarfed. (*Ministry of Healing*, page 290)

> "Those who make their dress a principal part of themselves, will, in general, become of no more value than their dress."
>
> William Hazlitt

Changing styles and elaborate, costly ornamentation squander the time and means of the rich, and lay waste the energies of mind and soul. They impose a heavy burden on the middle and poorer classes. Many who can hardly earn a livelihood, and who with simple modes might make their own clothing, are compelled to resort to the dressmaker in order to be in fashion. Many a poor girl, for the sake of a stylish gown, has deprived herself of warm underwear, and paid the penalty with her life. Many another, coveting the display and elegance of the rich, has been enticed into paths of dishonesty and shame. Many a home is deprived of comforts, many a man is driven to embezzlement or bankruptcy, to satisfy the extravagant demands of the wife or children. (*Ministry of Healing*, page 290)

Food for Thought

"Fashion is a form of ugliness so intolerable that we have to alter it every six months."

Oscar Wilde

An expensive dwelling, elaborate furnishings, display, luxury, and ease, do not furnish the conditions essential to a happy, useful life. (*Ministry of Healing*, page 365)

"How these vain ornaments, how these veils oppress me!"

Jean Racine

How much means is expended for things that are mere idols, things that engross thought and time and strength which should be put to a higher use! How much money is wasted on expensive houses and furniture, on selfish pleasures, luxurious and unwholesome food, hurtful indulgences! How much is squandered on gifts that benefit no one! (*Ministry of Healing*, page 207)

"A fashion is nothing but an induced epidemic."

George Bernard Shaw

STRENGTH

We cannot allow ourselves to act from impulse. We cannot be off guard for a moment. Beset with temptations without number, we must resist firmly or be conquered. Should we come to the close of life with our work undone, it would be an eternal loss. (*Ministry of Healing*, page 452)

Food for Thought

"Discipline is the soul of an army. It makes small numbers formidable; procures success to the weak, and esteem to all."

George Washington

"Firmness of purpose is one of the most necessary sinews of character, and one of the best instruments of success. Without it genius wastes its efforts in a maze of inconsistencies."

Philip Dormer Stanhope, Fourth Earl of Chesterfield

TEMPTATION

Not through the excitement or oblivion produced by unnatural or unhealthful stimulants; not through indulgence of the lower appetites or passions, is to be found true healing or refreshment for the body or the soul. Among the sick are many who are without God and without hope. They suffer from ungratified desires, disordered passions, and the condemnation of their own consciences; they are losing their hold upon this life, and they have no prospect for the life to come. Let not the attendants upon the sick hope to benefit these patients by granting them frivolous, exciting indulgences. These have been the curse of their lives. The hungry, thirsting soul will continue to hunger and thirst so long as it seeks to find satisfaction here. Those who drink at the fountain of selfish pleasure are deceived. They mistake hilarity for strength, and when the excitement ceases, their inspiration ends, and they are left to discontent and despondency. (*Ministry of Healing*, page 246)

Food for Thought

"While man's desires and aspirations stir he cannot choose but err."

Johann Wolfgang von Goethe

One of the most subtle and dangerous temptations that assail the children and youth in the cities is the love of pleasure. Holidays are numerous; games and horse racing draw thousands, and the whirl of excitement and pleasure attracts them away from the sober duties of life. Money that should have been saved for better uses is frittered away for amusements. (*Ministry of Healing*, page 364)

> "Now that adolescence is accessible to the multitude and not restricted to gentlemen and lords, many adults are taking alarm at what seems to be a barbaric horde of scruffy girls and boys out to dismantle the structure of society. It is hard to see any virtue in it at all. What the grown-ups see in its stead is considerable evidence of pride, covetousness, anger, gluttony, envy, sloth, and a great deal of lust."
>
> Louise J. Kaplan

The body is the only medium through which the mind and the soul are developed for the up-building of character. Hence it is that the adversary of souls directs his temptations to the enfeebling and degrading of the physical powers. His success here means the surrender to evil of the whole being. The tendencies of our physical nature, unless under the dominion of a higher power, will surely work ruin and death. (*Ministry of Healing*, page 130)

> "I count him braver who overcomes his desires than him who conquers his enemies, for the hardest victory is over self."
>
> Aristotle

Food for Thought

*I*t must be kept before the people that the right balance of the mental and moral powers depends in a great degree on the right condition of the physical system. By the indulgence of perverted appetite, man loses his power to resist temptation. (*Ministry of Healing,* page 335)

> "Temptations come, as a general rule, when they are sought."
>
> Margaret Oliphant

TOBACCO

*T*he use of tobacco is inconvenient, expensive, uncleanly, defiling to the user, and offensive to others. Its devotees are encountered everywhere. You rarely pass through a crowd but some smoker puffs his poisoned breath in your face. It is unpleasant and unhealthful to remain in a railway car or in a room where the atmosphere is laden with the fumes of liquor and tobacco. Though men persist in using these poisons themselves, what right have they to defile the air that others must breathe? (*Ministry of Healing,* page 328)

> "After years of denial and deception, the Philip Morris company has admitted that cigarette smoking causes lung cancer and other diseases. This formal acknowledgment comes far too late but still we must all welcome it. It can be the beginning of clearing the air."
>
> Bill Clinton

*B*oys begin the use of tobacco at a very early age. The habit thus formed when body and mind are especially susceptible to its

Food for Thought

effects, undermines the physical strength, dwarfs the body, stupefies the mind, and corrupts the morals. (*Ministry of Healing*, page 329)

> "Because children have unique vulnerabilities—they absorb greater concentrations of smoke than adults do from the same exposure—we must use greater caution in protecting them from environmental threats to their health. One of the ways parents and caregivers can do this is by taking the Smoke-Free Home Pledge—simply choosing not to smoke, and not letting others smoke, in your home or anywhere children are present. Of course, we encourage people to quit smoking entirely. We realize that is difficult, so until they can take that step, we ask that they smoke outside."
>
> Christine Todd Whitman

But what can be done to teach children and youth the evils of a practice of which parents, teachers, and ministers set them the example? Little boys, hardly emerged from babyhood, may be seen smoking their cigarettes. If one speaks to them about it, they say, "My father uses tobacco." They point to the minister or the Sunday-school superintendent and say, "Such a man smokes; what harm for me to do as he does?" Many workers in the temperance cause are addicted to the use of tobacco. What power can such persons have to stay the progress of intemperance? (*Ministry of Healing*, page 329)

> "Am I biting the hand that feeds me? If the hand that once fed me is the tobacco industry, then that hand has killed 10 million people and may kill millions more."
>
> Patrick Reynolds

Among children and youth the use of tobacco is working untold harm. The unhealthful practices of past generations affect the

Food for Thought

children and youth of today. Mental inability, physical weakness, disordered nerves, and unnatural cravings are transmitted as a legacy from parents to children. And the same practices, continued by the children, are increasing and perpetuating the evil results. To this cause in no small degree is owing the physical, mental, and moral deterioration which is becoming such a cause of alarm. (*Ministry of Healing*, page 328)

> "If you took 1,000 young adult smokers, one will be murdered, six will die on the roads, but 500 will die from tobacco."
>
> Sir Richard Peto

Tobacco is a slow, insidious, but most malignant poison. In whatever form it is used, it tells upon the constitution; it is all the more dangerous because its effects are slow and at first hardly perceptible. It excites and then paralyzes the nerves. It weakens and clouds the brain. Often it affects the nerves in a more powerful manner than does intoxicating drink. It is more subtle, and its effects are difficult to eradicate from the system. Its use excites a thirst for strong drink and in many cases lays the foundation for the liquor habit. (*Ministry of Healing*, page 327)

> "A custom loathsome to the eye, hateful to the nose, harmful to the brain, dangerous to the lungs, and in the black, stinking fume thereof nearest resembling the horrible Stygian smoke of the pit that is bottomless."
>
> King James I of England

Food for Thought

VICES

Many come under the physician's care who are ruining soul and body by the use of tobacco or intoxicating drink. The physician who is true to his responsibility must point out to these patients the cause of their suffering. But if he himself is a user of tobacco or intoxicants, what weight will be given to his words? With the consciousness of his own indulgence before him, will he not hesitate to point out the plague spot in the life of his patient? While using these things himself, how can he convince the youth of their injurious effects?
(*Ministry of Healing*, page 133)

> "If I knew and could master myself all other difficulties would vanish. To overcome long-settled habits, one has almost to change 'the stamp of nature'; but bad habits must be changed and good ones formed in their stead, or I shall never find the pearls I seek."
>
> Rutherford Birchard Hayes

The continued use of these nerve irritants is followed by headache, wakefulness, palpitation of the heart, indigestion, trembling, and many other evils; for they wear away the life forces. Tired nerves need rest and quiet instead of stimulation and overwork. Nature needs time to recuperate her exhausted energies. When her forces are goaded on by the use of stimulants, more will be accomplished for a time; but, as the system becomes debilitated by their constant use, it gradually becomes more difficult to rouse the energies to the desired point. The demand for stimulants becomes more difficult to control, until the will is overborne and there seems to be no power to deny the unnatural craving. (*Ministry of Healing*, page 326)

Food for Thought

> "In a word, coffee is the drunkard's settle-brain, the fool's pastime, who admires it for being the production of Asia, and is ravished with delight when he hears the berries grow in the deserts of Arabia, but would not give a farthing for a hogshead of it."
>
> — Thomas Tryon

While disordering his nerves and clouding his brain by the use of narcotic poisons, how can one be true to the trust reposed in him as a skillful physician? How impossible for him to discern quickly or to execute with precision! (*Ministry of Healing*, page 134)

> "Strength is the capacity to break a chocolate bar into four pieces with your bare hands—and then eat just one of the pieces"
>
> — Judith Viorst

Many persons bring disease upon themselves by their self-indulgence. They have not lived in accordance with natural law or the principles of strict purity. Others have disregarded the laws of health in their habits of eating and drinking, dressing, or working. Often some form of vice is the cause of feebleness of mind or body. Should these persons gain the blessing of health, many of them would continue to pursue the same course of heedless transgression of God's natural and spiritual laws, reasoning that if God heals them in answer to prayer, they are at liberty to continue their unhealthful practices. (*Ministry of Healing*, page 227)

> "The loose string, which is like a life of indulgence, produces a poor sound when struck."
>
> — Buddha

Tea acts as a stimulant and, to a certain extent, produces intoxication. The action of coffee and many other popular drinks

Food for Thought

is similar. The first effect is exhilarating. The nerves of the stomach are excited; these convey irritation to the brain, and this in turn is aroused to impart increased action to the heart and short-lived energy to the entire system. Fatigue is forgotten; the strength seems to be increased. The intellect is aroused, the imagination becomes more vivid. (*Ministry of Healing,* page 326)

> "The drink, which has come to supple the place of beer, has, in general, been tea. It is notorious, that tea has no useful strength in it; that it, besides being good for nothing, has badness in it, because it is well-known to produce want of sleep in many cases, and in all cases, to shake and weaken the nerves."
>
> William Cobbett

The world over, cities are becoming hotbeds of vice. On every hand are the sights and sounds of evil. Everywhere are enticements to sensuality and dissipation. The tide of corruption and crime is continually swelling. Every day brings the record of violence—robberies, murders, suicides, and crimes unnamable. (*Ministry of Healing,* page 363)

> "More people are flattered into virtue than bullied out of vice."
>
> Robert Smith Surtees

How can a physician stand in the community as an example of purity and self-control, how can he be an effectual worker in the temperance cause, while he himself is indulging a vile habit? How can he minister acceptably at the bedside of the sick and the dying, when his very breath is offensive, laden with the odor of liquor or tobacco? (*Ministry of Healing,* page 134)

Food for Thought

"Because of impatience we were driven out of Paradise, because of impatience we cannot return."

W.H. Auden

However skilled and faithful a physician may be, there is in his experience much of apparent discouragement and defeat. Often his work fails of accomplishing that which he longs to see accomplished. Though health is restored to his patients, it may be no real benefit to them or to the world. Many recover health, only to repeat the indulgences that invited disease. With the same eagerness as before, they plunge again into the round of self-indulgence and folly. The physician's work for them seems like effort thrown away. (*Ministry of Healing,* page 134)

"The pleasures of the world are deceitful; they promise more than they give. They trouble us in seeking them, they do not satisfy us when possessing them, and they make us despair in losing them."

Madame De Lambert

Great efforts are put forth, time and money and labor almost without limit are expended, in enterprises and institutions for reforming the victims of evil habits. And even these efforts are inadequate to meet the great necessity. Yet how small is the result! How few are permanently reclaimed! (*Ministry of Healing,* page 351)

"I feel the end approaching. Quick, bring me my dessert, coffee and liqueur."

Jean Anthelme Brillat-Savarin's great aunt Pierette

Food for Thought

WORKING DILIGENTLY

Attention should be given to the establishment of various industries so that poor families can find employment. Carpenters, blacksmiths, and indeed everyone who understands some line of useful labor, should feel a responsibility to teach and help the ignorant and the unemployed. (*Ministry of Healing*, page 194)

> "The habits of our whole species fall into three great classes—useful labor, useless labor, and idleness. Of these the first only is meritorious; and to it all the products of labor rightfully belong; but the two latter, while they exist, are heavy pensioners upon the first, robbing it of a large portion of its just rights. The only remedy for this is to, as far as possible, drive useless labor and idleness out of existence."
>
> Abraham Lincoln

Many transgress the laws of health through ignorance, and they need instruction. But the greater number know better than they do. They need to be impressed with the importance of making their knowledge a guide of life. The physician has many opportunities both of imparting a knowledge of health principles and of showing the importance of putting them in practice. By right instruction he can do much to correct evils that are working untold harm. (*Ministry of Healing*, page 126)

> "Sweat cleanses from the inside. It comes from places a shower will never reach."
>
> George Sheehan

We cannot be too often reminded that health does not depend on chance. It is a result of obedience to law. This is recognized

Food for Thought

by the contestants in athletic games and trials of strength. These men make the most careful preparation. They submit to thorough training and strict discipline. Every physical habit is carefully regulated. They know that neglect, excess, or carelessness, which weakens or cripples any organ or function of the body, would ensure defeat. (*Ministry of Healing*, page 128)

> "All labor that uplifts humanity has dignity and importance and should be undertaken with painstaking excellence."
>
> Dr. Martin Luther King, Jr.

Those who have overtaxed their physical powers should not be encouraged to forgo manual labor entirely. But labor, to be of the greatest advantage, should be systematic and agreeable. (*Ministry of Healing*, page 238)

> "Continual hard labor deadens the energies of the soul, and benumbs the faculties of the mind; the ideas become confined, the mind barren, and, like the scorching sands of Arabia, produces nothing; or, like the uncultivated soil, brings forth thorns and thistles. Again, continual hard labor irritates our tempers and sours our dispositions; the whole system becomes worn out with toil and fatigue; nature herself becomes almost exhausted, and we care but little whether we live or die."
>
> Maria Stewart

Light employment in useful labor, while it does not tax mind or body, has a happy influence upon both. It strengthens the muscles, improves the circulation, and gives the invalid the satisfaction of knowing that he is not wholly useless in this busy world. He may be able to do but little at first, but he will soon find his strength increasing, and the amount of work done can be increased accordingly. (*Ministry of Healing*, page 240)

Food for Thought

"One of the symptoms of an approaching nervous breakdown is the belief that one's work is terribly important."

Bertrand Russell

Many who till the soil fail to secure adequate returns because of their neglect. Their orchards are not properly cared for, the crops are not put in at the right time, and a mere surface work is done in cultivating the soil. Their ill success they charge to the unproductiveness of the land. False witness is often borne in condemning land that, if properly worked, would yield rich returns. The narrow plans, the little strength put forth, the little study as to the best methods, call loudly for reform. (*Ministry of Healing,* page 193)

"If I had six hours to chop down a tree, I'd spend the first hour sharpening the ax."

Abraham Lincoln

The same spirit and principles that one brings into the daily labor will be brought into the whole life. Those who desire a fixed amount to do and a fixed salary, and who wish to prove an exact fit without the trouble of adaptation or training, are not the ones whom God calls to work in His cause. Those who study how to give as little as possible of their physical, mental, and moral power are not the workers upon whom He can pour out abundant blessings. Their example is contagious. Self-interest is the ruling motive. Those who need to be watched and who work only as every duty is specified to them, are not the ones who will be pronounced good and faithful. Workers are needed who manifest energy, integrity, diligence, those who are willing to do anything that needs to be done. (*Ministry of Healing,* page 499)

Note from the Editor

When mining for valuable ore or seeking perfect crystals, prospectors often unearth many tons of dirt and rock to gather just a single ounce of gold, or collect one very precious gem.

    The number of words in this book represents less than one-fifth of one percent of the total number of words written and published by Ellen G. White during her lifetime. After careful exploration, while searching for diamonds, rubies, and sapphires, I excerpted each one of these quotations from the *Ministry of Healing*, originally published in 1905. I recommend reading *Ministry of Healing* and White's other works in their entirety, for her collective writings represent a full range of the best of humankind's philosophical thought.

—Robert Cohen

OTHER SQUAREONE TITLES OF INTEREST

GOD'S NUTRITIONIST
Pearls of Wisdom from Ellen G. White
Edited by Robert Cohen

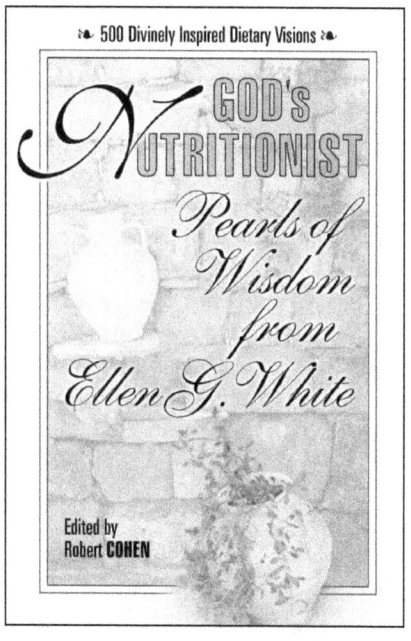

As a spiritual leader, prolific writer, and pioneering nutritionist of the nineteenth and twentieth centuries, Ellen G. White had a profound effect on millions of people around the world. Today, her words continue to guide and inspire countless individuals. Although she is the most translated author in the history of American literature, few people outside the Seventh-day Adventist Church have known of her work—that is, until now. In this unique book, Robert Cohen presents Ellen White's most insightful quotations on health and nutrition, and supports them with current scientific facts that confirm her views.

Here are 500 of White's "pearls of wisdom"—words that are as practical, insightful, and moral as they are accurate. Gathered from her many works, these classic quotations beautifully present her beliefs, from her stand as an ardent vegetarian to her view of the negative effects of dairy products on health. To this, Cohen has added fascinating excerpts culled from today's leading scientific journals, validating the many points made by Mrs. White.

Whether viewed as a unique slice of history, a book of prophetic wisdom, or a relevant guide to everyday life, *God's Nutritionist* offers both a beacon of light and a path of truth.

$16.95 • 192 pages • 5.5 x 8.5-inch quality paperback • ISBN 978-0-7570-0146-8

Going Wild in the Kitchen
The Fresh & Sassy Tastes of Vegetarian Cooking
Leslie Cerier

Going Wild in the Kitchen provides helpful cooking tips and techniques. The book contains over 150 kitchen-tested recipes for healthful, taste-tempting dishes—creative masterpieces that contain such unique ingredients as edible flowers; sea vegetables; and wild mushrooms, berries, and herbs. It encourages the creative side of novice and seasoned cooks alike, prompting them to follow their instincts and "go wild" in the kitchen by adding, changing, or substituting ingredients in existing recipes. To help, a wealth of suggestions is found throughout. A list of organic foods sources completes this user-friendly cookbook.

$16.95 • 240 pages • 7.5 x 9-inch quality paperback • ISBN 978-0-7570-0091-1

Eat Smart Eat Raw
Creative Vegetarian Recipes for a Healthier Life
Kate Wood

From healing diseases to detoxifying your body, from lowering cholesterol to eliminating excess weight, the many important health benefits derived from a raw vegetarian diet are too important to ignore. However, now there is another compelling reason to go raw—taste! In her new book *Eat Smart, Eat Raw*, cook and health writer Kate Wood not only explains how to get started, but also provides delicious kitchen-tested recipes guaranteed to surprise and delight even the fussiest of eaters.

Eat Smart, Eat Raw begins by explaining the basics of cooking without heat, from choosing the best equipment to stocking your pantry. What follows are twelve recipe chapters filled with truly exceptional dishes, including hearty breakfasts, savory soups, satisfying entrées, and luscious desserts.

$15.95 • 184 pages • 7.5 x 9-inch quality paperback • ISBN 978-0-7570-0261-8

As You Like It Cookbook
Imaginative Gourmet Dishes with Exciting Vegetarian Options
Ron Pickarski

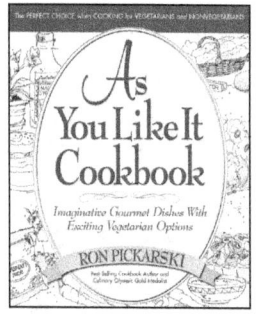

When it comes to food, we certainly like to have it our way. However, catering to individual tastes can pose quite a challenge for the cook. The *As You Like It Cookbook* is designed to help you meet the challenge of cooking for both vegetarians and nonvegetarians alike. It offers over 170 great-tasting dishes that cater to a broad range of tastes. Many of the easy-to-follow recipes are vegetarian—and offer ingredient alternatives for meat eaters. Conversely, recipes that include meat, poultry, or fish offer nonmeat ingredient options. Furthermore, if the recipe includes eggs or dairy products, a vegan alternative is provided. This book has it all—delicious breakfast favorites, satisfying soups and sandwiches, mouth-watering entrées, and delectable desserts.

$16.95 • 216 pages • 7.5 x 9-inch quality paperback • ISBN 978-0-7570-0013-3

Enemy of the Steak
Vegetarian Recipes to Win Friends and Influence Meat-Eaters
Nikki & David Goldbeck

Enemy of the Steak first presents basic information on vegetarian cooking and stocking the vegetarian pantry. Then eight great chapters offer recipes for breakfast fare; appetizers and hors d'oeuvres; soups; salads; entrées; side dishes; sauces, toppings, and marinades; and desserts. Throughout the book, the Goldbecks have included practical tips and advice on weight loss, disease prevention, and other important topics. They also offer dozens of fascinating facts about why fruits and veggies are so good for you.

A perfect marriage of nutrition and the art of cooking, *Enemy of the Steak* is for everyone who loves a good healthy meal. Simply put, it's great food for smart people. If you have to take sides, you couldn't be in better company.

$16.95 • 248 pages • 7.5 x 9-inch quality paperback • ISBN 978-0-7570-0273-1

JUICE ALIVE
The Ultimate Guide to Juicing Remedies
Steven Baily, ND, and Larry Trivieri, Jr.

The book begins with a look at the history of juicing. It then examines the many components that make fresh juice truly good for you—good for weight loss and so much more. Next, it offers practical advice about the types of juices available, as well as buying and storing tips for produce. The second half of the book begins with an important chart that matches up common ailments with the most appropriate juices, followed by over 100 delicious juice recipes. Let *Juice Alive* introduce you to a world bursting with the incomparable tastes and benefits of fresh juice.

$14.95 • 272 pages • 6 x 9-inch quality paperback • ISBN 978-0-7570-0266-3

GREENS AND GRAINS ON THE DEEP BLUE SEA COOKBOOK
Fabulous Vegetarian Cuisine from the Holistic Holiday at Sea Cruises
Sandy Pukel and Mark Hanna

Each of the book's more than 120 kitchen-tested recipes has been designed to provide not only great taste, but also maximum nutrition. Choose from among an innovative selection of taste-tempting appetizers, soups, salads, entrées, side dishes, and desserts. Easy-to-follow instructions ensure that even the novice cook will have superb results. With *Greens and Grains on the Deep Blue Sea Cookbook,* you can enjoy fabulous signature dishes from the Holistic Holiday at Sea cruises whenever you desire—in the comfort of your own home.

$16.95 • 160 pages • 7.5 x 9-inch quality paperback • ISBN 978-0-7570-0287-8

For more information about our books, visit our website at www.squareonepublishers.com

www.ingramcontent.com/pod-product-compliance
Lightning Source LLC
Chambersburg PA
CBHW071920290426
44110CB00013B/1423